CBT Toolbox for Teens

101 Exercises for Adolescents to Beat Anxiety, Manage Stress, and Boost Mental Well-Being

© Copyright 2023 - All rights reserved.

The content contained within this book may not be reproduced, duplicated, or transmitted without direct written permission from the author or the publisher.

Under no circumstances will any blame or legal responsibility be held against the publisher or author for any damages, reparation, or monetary loss due to the information contained within this book, either directly or indirectly.

Legal Notice:

This book is copyright-protected. It is only for personal use. You cannot amend, distribute, sell, use, quote, or paraphrase any part of the content within this book without the consent of the author or publisher.

Disclaimer Notice:

Please note the information contained within this document is for educational and entertainment purposes only. All effort has been executed to present accurate, up-to-date, reliable, and complete information. No warranties of any kind are declared or implied. Readers acknowledge that the author is not engaging in the rendering of legal, financial, medical, or professional advice. The content within this book has been derived from various sources. Please consult a licensed professional before attempting any techniques outlined in this book.

By reading this document, the reader agrees that under no circumstances is the author responsible for any losses, direct or indirect, that are incurred as a result of the use of the information contained within this document, including, but not limited to, errors, omissions, or inaccuracies.

Table of Contents

LETTER TO THE PARENT 1
LETTER TO THE TEENAGER 3
SECTION 1: HOW CAN CBT HELP ME? 4
SECTION 2: THOUGHTS, EMOTIONS, AND BEHAVIORS 14
SECTION 3: TAMING ANXIETY 24
SECTION 4: FACING MY FEAR 31
SECTION 5: OVERCOMING MENTAL FILTERING 43
SECTION 6: BEATING THE BLUES 52
SECTION 7: CONTROLLING ANGER 62
SECTION 8: MY SELF-ESTEEM 73
SECTION 9: NO MORE "SHOULDS" 92
SECTION 10: PEACE WITHIN YOU 99
BONUS SECTION: MY BEHAVIOR LOG 106
THANK YOU 108
CHECK OUT ANOTHER BOOK IN THE SERIES 109
REFERENCES 110

Letter to the Parent

Dear Parent,

Talking with teenagers can sometimes be challenging because they feel that their parents don't understand their struggles. They are also in a critical age where they are neither kids nor grownups. They don't want to ask for help, but they also can't handle certain things by themselves. Show your child that you understand what they are going through by giving them this book. It will give them the independence they need to tackle their issues while keeping you involved to provide guidance and assistance.

Your teenager can learn to control their thoughts, emotions, and behavior through the power of cognitive-behavioral therapy or CBT. Understandably, this is a new concept for your child. For this reason, the book introduces it in detail while highlighting how it manages intense emotions like phobias, anger, and anxiety.

Once your child grasps what CBT is and what it can do for them, they can learn certain aspects about themselves, like the relationship between their thoughts, emotions, and behavior and how each one can influence the other. This is significant information they should understand before they begin to apply CBT to their lives.

One of the main reasons you have probably decided to give your child this book is to help them with their anxiety. Anxiety is common among teens, but many don't recognize what they are going through or how it impacts their lives. The book explains this concept in detail with its symptoms and factors. Sometimes anxiety can be crippling, and your child can feel there is no escape from these emotions. However, the book manages to give them a glimmer of hope, letting them now that they aren't alone and that they can overcome it with CBT.

Fear is another issue that your child is struggling with and doesn't know what to do about it. As a parent, you understand how this emotion can be damaging to their self-esteem. Often, fear is irrational and stems from negative thoughts. Your child will learn here about their fears and how they can face and defeat them.

Negative thoughts change the way people see themselves and the world around them. You have probably experienced them firsthand; who hasn't? All parents wish they could protect their children from these thoughts so they could only see the good things in life. Similar to fear, negative thoughts can also be irrational. Your child will learn here how these thoughts affect them and how they are only focusing on the negatives while ignoring the positives.

It is heartbreaking watching your child going through depression. Since it is a sensitive issue, it can be tough to discuss it with them. Although this book isn't by any means a substitute for a therapist, it explains in a calm and friendly tone the concept of depression and its symptoms. It is necessary for your child to understand if they are depressed or just sad. Knowing the difference will give them a better understanding of what they are experiencing.

Anger has always been associated with teenagers. You have probably heard from family or friends that "Teens are angry all the time; it isn't just you." While anger is a natural emotion, it isn't normal for a person to be "angry all the time." The book explains to your child that the negative emotions they may be experiencing are the result of their anger. They will also learn about triggers so they can get to the root of their anger issues and control their explosive emotions.

Low self-esteem is another common issue among many teenagers. They can't help but compare themselves to many people their age. One can't forget the unrealistic beauty standards set by social media. Your child will learn how to change their thoughts so they can see themselves in a better light.

Do you remember when you were a teenager and had to do the things because you should rather than the things you want? People live according to certain rules, and sometimes, they forget to do what they love and enjoy. Your child needs to learn the stressful impact of all the "shoulds," identify their values, and change how they view these rules.

Don't you wish your teen was calm and at peace? This isn't impossible. There are certain strategies that they can implement that will make them feel relaxed and quiet their angry and negative thoughts.

Each chapter has a variety of fun and practical exercises and techniques based on Cognitive Behavioral Therapy (CBT) to empower teens. This book has all the information your child needs to begin their healing journey. It will be their guide every step of the way, and you will start to notice its impact on them.

However, this book is not a substitute for professional help. You must seek guidance from mental health professionals if your teenagers' challenges persist or worsen.

Letter to the Teenager

Hey there,

There is no denying that teenagers don't have it easy. More often than not, you feel alone and that no one understands you. You are under pressure at school and home and sometimes feel like you don't fit in anywhere. It's OK to feel this way, and you aren't alone. Your friends and many other teenagers feel this way, too. Your parents and your teachers did when they were your age. In fact, people of all ages experience stress and anxiety at some time in their lives.

Choosing to seek help is courageous and a step that will change your life. This book will be your guide and friend through this journey. It includes exercises and techniques that are fun and effective. They will change the way you think and feel about many things in life and provide you with methods to manage your stress, anxiety, and depression.

You are stronger than you think and have the power to change your life. Everything in life is a choice, even healing and positive changes. Making the decision to be and do better is brave. Take the first step today and get ready to meet a new you when you finish this book.

Section 1: How Can CBT Help Me?

CBT, or Cognitive Behavioral Therapy, is a type of talking therapy that includes many strategies, coping skills, and exercises to treat anxiety, depression, anger, grief, fears, and other issues. It focuses on the relationship between your thoughts, attitudes, and beliefs – and how they affect your actions and emotions.

In other words, your thoughts determine how you will feel and react in every situation. For instance, you and your teammates lost a big soccer match. This is upsetting. However, if you only focus on the loss, you will be disappointed and angry at yourself and your teammates. If you focus on how hard you and your teammates played and gave it your all, you will see it as an opportunity to learn from your mistakes and do better next time. This way, you will feel sad about the loss but won't be angry, and you're more likely to learn from your mistakes with this attitude; an angry attitude hinders your motivation.

CBT helps you develop better ways to deal with negative emotions.
https://www.pexels.com/photo/silver-iphone-6-987585/

CBT makes you aware of your negative thoughts or behavior towards a situation so you can develop different and better ways to behave and think. For instance, if you have a phobia of closed spaces, CBT can make you change the way you think and feel about them. Instead of being afraid, CBT will teach you how to change your perspective and that there is nothing scary about closed spaces, so you can feel safe and relaxed.

Benefits and Goals of CBT

- It provides results in a short amount of time.
- You don't need a therapist; you can practice these techniques alone at home.
- It treats a variety of intense emotions and negative behaviors.
- It teaches you to recognize and take control of unhelpful thoughts and change them to positive ones.
- You will also learn to think logically and realistically to challenge irrational negative thoughts.
- It boosts your self-esteem.
- You will learn problem-solving skills.
- It teaches you to identify and manage intense emotions.
- It provides you with coping skills to manage stress and anxiety.
- It teaches you to cope with grief and loss.
- It reduces your stress and teaches you different ways to relax and unwind.
- It teaches you to control your anger and healthily express your emotions.
- It treats depression and changes your behavior to a happy and upbeat person.
- It is one of the most common treatments against many types of anxiety, like phobias and social anxiety. You will learn how to challenge the thoughts making you anxious and face your fears. These techniques will show that your thoughts and fears aren't as bad or scary as you think.
- The skills you learn will benefit you for the rest of your life.
- It shows you that you can change and get better as soon as you believe you can.

Does CBT Work?

You are probably thinking, "This is too good to be true; does it actually work?" The short answer is yes, it does. Many children, teens, and adults swear by this technique.

Jessica, 12

Jessica was a happy girl who worked hard in school and always got good grades. However, when her parents divorced, she started acting out at home and school. Her parents took her to a therapist, and she told him that she was angry at her mom and dad for getting a divorce and destroying her family. The therapist used CBT techniques to change how Jessica thought of her parent's divorce. He showed her that they still loved her and are much happier now. He also taught her to recognize her negative thoughts and healthily express her feelings. After three months, she stopped acting out, accepted her parent's divorce, and went back to her old self.

Questions to Reflect on

1. Do I have negative thoughts?

   _____

   _____

2. What are these thoughts about?

   _____

   _____

   _____

3. Are my emotions out of control?

   _____

   _____

4. Am I ready to change my thoughts and manage my emotions?

   _____

   _____

Exercises

1. Journaling

Write down every negative thought or emotion you experienced throughout the day. Use smiley faces to describe how intense each one is.

2. Opinion or Fact

1. Think of your thoughts about yourself, like "My friends hate me" or "I won't get good grades."
2. In this worksheet, write which ones are facts and which are opinions. In other words, how realistic are your thoughts? Are you basing them on facts, or are they personal beliefs?

FACT OR OPINION

Facts are veriable statements. Opinions are personal interpretations of facts, which differ from person to person. For example, it is a fact that the sky is blue, and an opinion that the weather is beautiful.

Despite knowing the difference between facts and opinions, your brain does not always differentiate between the two. Harmful opinions, such as "I'm a bad person," are sometimes treated as fact. Even without evidence, these opinions may contribute to negative thinking, stress, and other problems.

Instructions: With practice, you can get better at spotting the difference between fact and opinion. Read each of the statements below and identify if they are fact or opinion

	Statement	Fact	Opinion
1.	I listened to my friend talk about their bad day.		
2.	I am a good friend.		
3.	I am ugly.		
4.	I have a blemish on my face.		
5.	My hair looks bad.		
6.	My boss said that I did a great job on the project.		
7.	No one will ever like me.		
8.	My crush said "no" when I asked them out.		
9.	I'm not as smart as the rest of my class.		
10.	I'm lazy.		
11.	I watched TV instead of doing my homework.		
12.	My friend is angry at me. I know this because they were frowning.		
13.	My friend frowned.		
14.	Everyone was bored during my speech.		
15.	I should always be nice.		

3. Worrying vs. Reality

Similar to the previous exercise, think of everything you are worried about and ask yourself, how likely are these things to happen? Write the most likely scenarios under reality and the least likely ones under worrying in the worksheet.

What Could Happen vs. What Will Happen

"When anxiety takes hold, it's often effortless to envision the most dire scenarios imaginable. However, it's crucial to recognize that these apprehensions may never materialize. The realm of possibility isn't synonymous with certainty."

What is something you are worried about?

Thinking about what will happen, instead of what could happen, can help you worry less. Whenever you start to worry, answer these questions:

What are some clues that your worry will not come true?

If your worry does not come true, what will probably happen instead?

If your worry does come true, how will you handle it? Will you eventually be okay?

After answering these questions, how has your worry changed?

---

4. Core Beliefs

Write down all your core beliefs about yourself, family, friends, school, and the world around you. You need to discover your beliefs to prepare yourself for the coming chapters.

5. Pros and Cons

Write down a particularly negative thought or belief you can't get out of your head in this worksheet, then write the pros and cons of having these thoughts/beliefs.

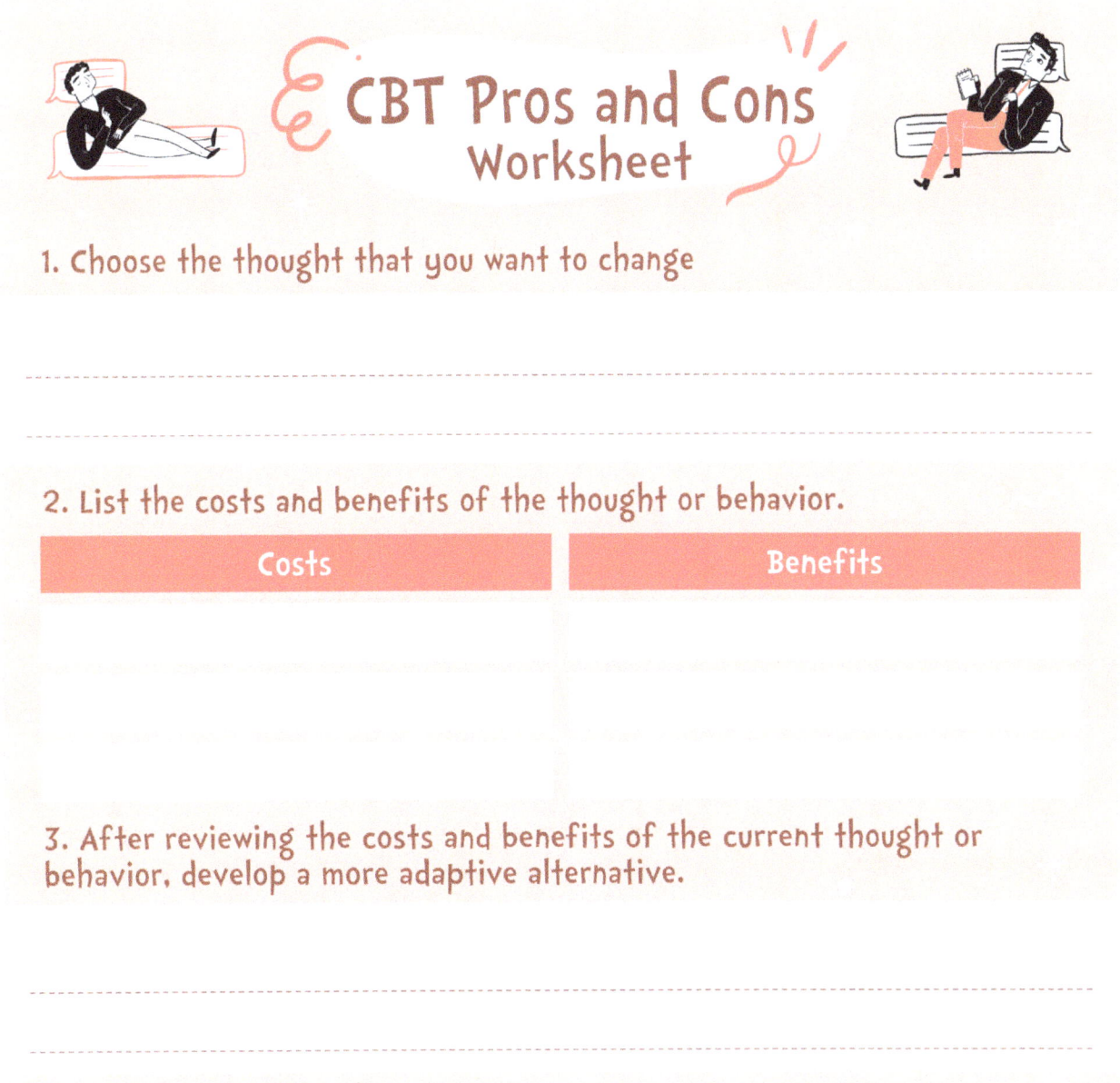

6. Catching the Negative Thoughts

Ask your friends and family what they really think of you and write it down. Next, read them out loud and see which of their opinions contradict your negative thoughts.

7. Problem-Solving Skills

Write down one of your biggest problems and come up with three solutions for it.

The Problem

The Solutions

1.

2.

3.

8. Negative Thoughts

Write down three situations where your negative thoughts held you back in life, and next to each one, write what you wish you had done differently.

1.

2.

3.

9. Negative Feelings

In this worksheet, write down some of your negative feelings like anger and stress, then write the consequences of each one, whether something that had already happened, like yelling at your siblings when you are angry, or what you imagine would happen. Then, write how you wish you would have handled the situation differently.

CHALLENGING NEGATIVE THOUGHTS

Depression, poor self-esteem, and anxiety are often the result of irrational negative thoughts. Someone who regularly receives positive feedback at work might feel that they are horrible at their job because of one criticism. Their irrational thought about job performance will dictate how they feel about themselves. Challenging irrational thoughts can help us change them.

Answer the following questions to assess your thought:

✳ Is there substantial evidence for my thought?

✳ Is there evidence contrary to my thought?

✳ Am I attempting to interpret this situation without all the evidence?

✳ What would a friend think about this situation?

✳ If I look at the situation positively, how is it different?

✳ Will this matter a year from now? How about five years from now?

10. Check in on Yourself

After exposing yourself to your negative emotions and thoughts, pause for a couple of minutes and check in on yourself. Write down how you are feeling mentally, emotionally, and physically.

_____

_____

_____

Section 2: Thoughts, Emotions, and Behaviors

The cognitive triangle shows how thoughts, emotions, and behaviors affect one another. This means changing your thoughts will change how you feel and behave.

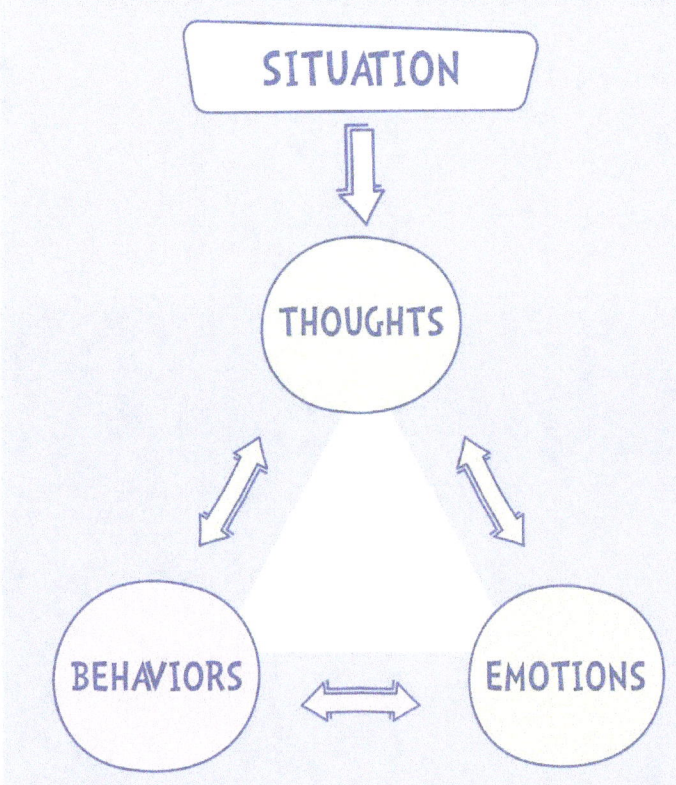

A SITUATION is anything that happens in your life, which triggers the cognitive triangle.

THOUGHTS are your interpretations of a situation. For example, if a stranger looks at you with an angry expression, you could think: "Oh no, what did I do wrong?" or "Maybe they are having a bad day."

EMOTIONS are feelings, such as happy, sad, angry, or worried. Emotions can have physical components as well as mental, such as low energy when feeling sad, or a stomachache when nervous.

BEHAVIORS are your response to a situation. Behaviors include actions such as saying something or doing something (or, choosing not to do something).

The cognitive triangle is a diagram that illustrates the relationship between your behavior, emotions, and thoughts.

Understanding Your Emotions

Behavior

Behavior reflects your actions in every situation. You change things, keep them the same, or make something happen. Your behavior can be external towards your surroundings or the people in your life, or internal through your feelings and thoughts.

Emotions

Emotions are how you feel about every situation you face in your life. For instance, you feel happy when you pass an exam, excited on your birthday, and sad when a loved one gets sick.

Thoughts

Thoughts are your beliefs and opinions about yourself, the world, and the people in your life. They can be positive or negative and can be so powerful that they change your personality. For instance, negative thoughts can make you angry and unhappy, while positive ones make you happy and upbeat.

Paying attention to your fleeting thoughts helps you understand and manage your emotions.
https://pxhere.com/en/photo/1189903

Your thoughts, emotions, and behavior are connected. Your emotions often reflect your thoughts, while both influence your behavior. For example, if you have negative thoughts about school, you will also develop negative emotions towards it and behave badly by acting out or not studying. Your emotions also affect your thoughts. If you feel sad or angry, you will have negative thoughts which will influence your behavior.

If you change one of them, the others will follow. For instance, if you have positive thoughts, you will feel happy and behave pleasantly.

"Thoughts create emotions, emotions create feelings, and feelings create behavior. So our thoughts must be positive to attract the right people, events, and circumstances into our lives." *Avis Williams.*

However, this isn't always easy, especially if you are consumed with automated thoughts. They are the negative and irrational beliefs you aren't aware of and can become your natural response to different situations. For example, you fail a test and react by thinking, *"I am a failure and will never amount to anything."*

These thoughts trigger negative emotions and make you feel scared, angry, anxious, sad, guilty, or ashamed. Naturally, these emotions will affect your behavior as well.

You should always pay attention to your emotional responses. Notice how every situation makes you feel. Are you sad, frustrated, irritated, or angry? Learning the names of different emotions is a great way to communicate how you feel.

Exercises

11. Venn Diagram

In this diagram, write down specific thoughts, emotions, and behaviors. Observe where they intersect, indicating the interdependence between these components.

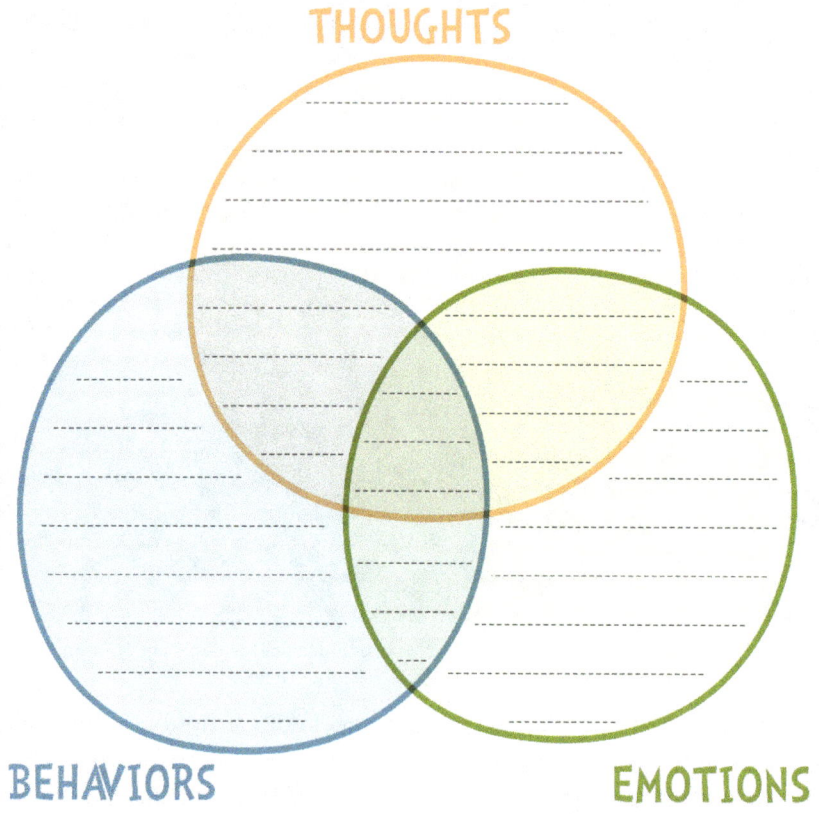

12. One Leads to Another

Write about an event or situation that triggered certain thoughts, emotions, and behaviors.

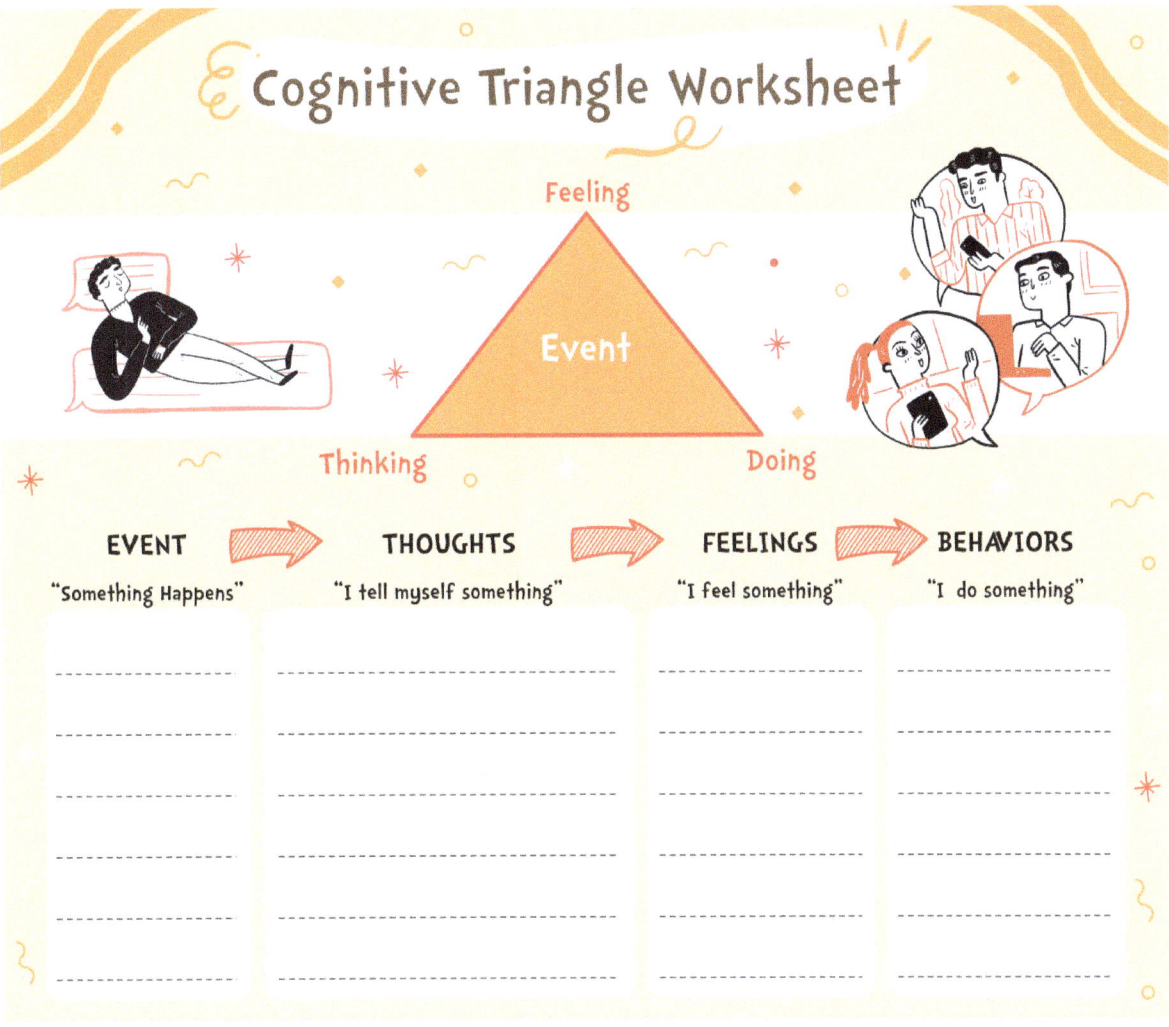

13. Emotional Vocabulary

Check the emotions in this worksheet and circle the ones you experienced in the last month.

List of Emotions

- Amazed
- Angry
- Annoyed
- Anxious
- Ashamed
- Bitter
- Bored
- Comfortable
- Confused
- Content
- Depressed
- Determined
- Disdain
- Disgusted
- Eager
- Embarrassed
- Energetic
- Envious
- Excited
- Foolish
- Frustrated
- Furious
- Grievous
- Happy
- Hopeful
- Hurt
- Inadequate
- Insecure
- Inspired
- Irritated
- Jealous
- Joy
- Lonely
- Lost
- Loving
- Miserable
- Motivated
- Nervous
- Overwhelmed
- Peaceful
- Proud
- Relieved
- Resentful
- Sad
- Satisfied
- Scared
- Self-conscious
- Shocked
- Silly
- Stupid
- Suspicious
- Tense
- Terrified
- Trapped
- Uncomfortable
- Worried
- Worthless

14. Recognize Automatic Thoughts

Fill this worksheet with different automatic thoughts you have experienced and their triggers, and replace them with new and positive ones.

For instance

- You didn't score in the last soccer game (Trigger)
- "My coach will kick me off the team because I am a failure." (Automatic thought)
- "I am a good player, and my coach knows it. I just made one mistake; he will understand." (New positive thought)

Our thoughts control how we feel about ourselves and the world around us. Positive thoughts lead to us feeling good and negative thoughts can put us down. Sometimes our thoughts happen so quickly that we fail to notice them, but they can still affect our mood. These are called automatic thoughts.

Oftentimes, our automatic thoughts are negative and irrational. Identifying these negative automatic thoughts and replacing them with new rational thoughts can improve our mood.

TRIGGER	AUTOMATIC THOUGHT	NEW THOUGHT
EXAMPLE: I made a mistake at work.	"I'm probably going to be fired. I always mess up. This is it. I'm no good at this job."	"I messed up, but mistakes happen. I'm going to work through this, like I always do."

15. Record Automatic Thoughts

Every time you experience an automatic thought like "I am going to fail this test," write it down. You should also include the situation, how these thoughts made you feel, and how you behaved.

16. Challenge These Thoughts

After you record your thoughts, write down why you think they are true and why they aren't. Read what you wrote aloud, then consider adding new positive thoughts to challenge the current ones.

17. Role-Play

Role-play various negative scenarios with your siblings, friends, or parents and notice the first thought that often comes to mind. They are most likely your automatic thoughts, so write them down to keep track of them.

Role-playing allows you to express different emotions and scenarios and their outcomes.
Julianne Zvalo-Martyn, CC BY-SA 4.0 <https://creativecommons.org/licenses/by-sa/4.0>, via Wikimedia Commons https://commons.wikimedia.org/wiki/File:Students_engaged_in_role_play.jpg

18. Cognitive Triangle

1. Inside the triangle, write down a tough situation you have been through lately.
2. Then, write your emotions, thoughts, and behavior during this situation.
3. Change your thoughts, emotions, or behavior to something positive. Write down how this will affect the other two and the situation's outcome.

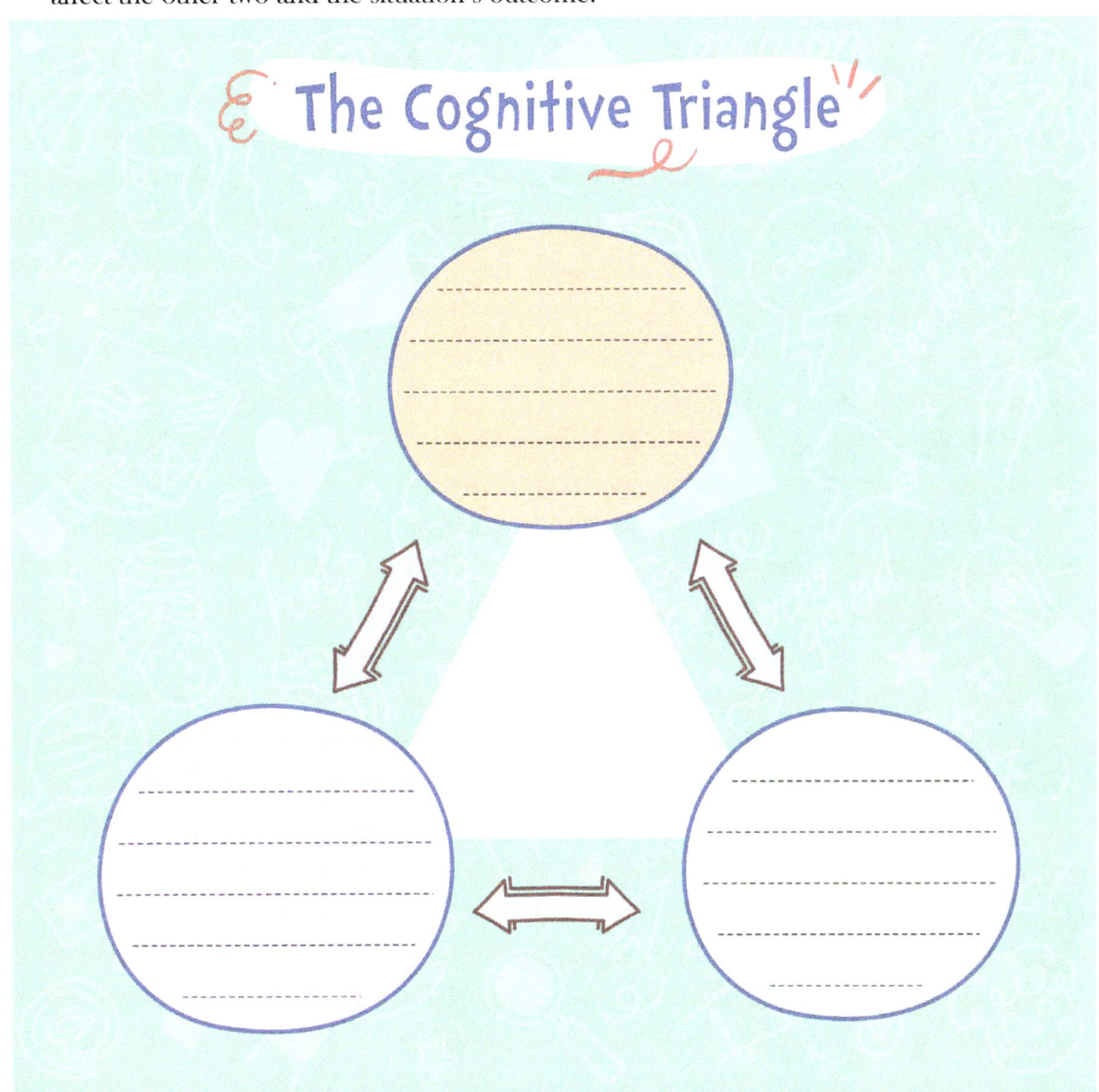

19. Thoughts Change

In this worksheet, write down a couple of situations that happened to you in the past and how they made you feel at the time. Now, reflect on these situations and write how you feel about them now compared to before. This exercise shows that you think differently with a clear head when time has passed, and your emotions have cooled down.

20. Emotional Charades

To better understand emotional responses, play emotional charades with your friends and family, where one acts a certain emotion and the other guesses it.

Section 3: Taming Anxiety

Anxiety is having a physical and mental reaction to various situations. If you have anxiety, you may not be aware of it. People use many words to describe this emotion, like feeling uneasy, on edge, worried, anguished, nervous, or having panic attacks. So, if you use any of these words to describe how you feel, you may suffer from anxiety.

Anxiety can creep up on you at any moment.
https://www.pexels.com/photo/photo-of-a-woman-crouching-while-her-hands-are-on-her-head-5542968/

Causes of Anxiety

- Stress
- Abuse
- Being bullied
- Trauma
- Loneliness and isolation
- Losing a loved one
- Constantly worrying about things that you have no control over, like earthquakes
- Pressure in school
- Seeing your parents going through financial problems or losing their jobs

Symptoms of Anxiety

- Uncontrollable worry
- Avoiding all anxiety triggers
- Having stomach problems
- Inability to sleep
- Only focusing on what's making you worried and failing to think about anything else
- Trouble concentrating at school
- Exhaustion
- Trembling
- Sweating
- Rapid breathing
- Fast heartbeat
- Panic attacks
- Feeling tense and nervous

There are certain thoughts, behaviors, and situations that escalate your anxiety. CBT reveals them to you so you can unmask specific patterns and triggers.

An Example of Using CBT to Overcome Anxiety

Justin struggled with anxiety all his life. He felt there was a war going on inside his head, and he couldn't quiet these thoughts. He tried CBT and breathing exercises whenever his thoughts were overwhelming. In time, he learned to cope with his anxiety and calm himself down.

Exercises

21. Track Your Pattern

To learn about your anxiety triggers, keep track of all "What if scenarios," intense emotions, and your behavior. You can carry a notebook, write them down immediately, and reflect on them at the end of the day to understand your anxiety pattern.

22. NO

Each time your mind wanders to negative "What-if scenarios," say out loud or under your breath, "No" or "Stop." This will interrupt the thought and bring you back to reality. Or you can use the "Shhh" technique like Captain America; Chris Evans once said, *"'Shhh' has been a big thing for me. It's so funny how noisy my brain is—and everyone's brain is noisy because that's what it does; it makes thoughts."*

Saying "No" can interrupt negative thoughts.
https://www.pexels.com/photo/person-holding-an-alphabet-4439408/

23. Feelings Change

1. Remember that feelings of anxiety won't last forever. So whenever you feel anxious, write down, "I am really worried right now, but it's OK. These feelings will go away, and I will feel calmer."
2. Now, imagine how you will feel when your emotions change, and write that down.

24. Act Normal

Whenever you experience anxiety in a non-threatening situation, let your anxiety know that you don't need it now by acting normally.

- Take deep breaths
- Have an open posture
- Smile
- Speak calmly

This way, your body lets your mind know there is nothing to worry about, and it should be relaxed. You can also chew gum since people don't do this when they are under threat.

25. Follow Your Train of Thought

Whenever you feel anxious about a situation, follow your train of thought. For example:

I don't want to speak up in class.

Why?

Because I am afraid people will laugh at me.

What will happen if they laugh at me?

This will hurt my feelings.

Have my classmates ever laughed at me before?

No.

So why would they laugh this time?

By following the train of thought, you can challenge it and prove it isn't based on anything real.

26. Repeat Affirmations

- This feeling will pass, and I will feel great again
- I can overcome my anxiety
- I am in control of my emotions
- I am capable and strong
- I trust myself

27. Breathing Exercise for Panic Attacks

Instructions:

1. Take a deep breath through your nostrils and fill your stomach with air.
2. Open your mouth and stick your tongue out.
3. Breathe out while roaring like a lion, or just say, "Ahh."
4. Repeat until you calm down.

28. 4-4-4-4 Breathing Exercise for Panic Attacks

Instructions:

1. Take a long, deep breath through your nostrils while counting to four.
2. Hold it and count to four.
3. Gently breathe out while counting to four.
4. Then pause and count to four.
5. Repeat until you feel calm.

29. Reframing Thoughts

Anxiety focuses on negative "What-if" scenarios. You can reframe these thoughts; instead of asking, "What if things go wrong?" try, "What if they went well?" For instance, you are worried about a test and keep thinking, "What if I fail?" "What if the test is hard?" "What if I panic and can't answer?" Adjust your thoughts by asking the opposite of these questions: "What if I pass?" What if the test is easy?" "What if I'm relaxed and answer all the questions?"

This technique allows you to interrupt negative thoughts with helpful ones that you can use to manage your anxiety.

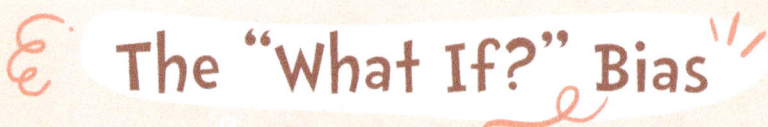

The "What If?" Bias

We often get caught up thinking about all the potential bad outcomes of a situation or decision, rather than adopting a rational perspective. This exercise can help you combat the "What If?" Bias to regain a balanced perspective and avoid catastrophizing.

Thinking of a situation or challenge that you'd like to tackle, use this worksheet to list both positive and negative "What Ifs?" in each of the columns.

Two examples are provided to get you started.

"What If" It's Negative?	"What If?" It's Positive?
E.g. What if I have a panic attack on stage?	E.g. What if I give the performance of my life?

30. Subjective Units of Distress Scale

Think of the last time you experienced anxiety and rate it from one to ten. Then, write in the empty spaces what triggered your anxiety and how to cope with this feeling.

Feelings of distress are subjective, meaning the experience of distress is influenced by personal feelings, tastes, or opinions. As such, we need a method to communicate with one another how much distress you're experiencing. The subjective units of distress scale (referred to as "SUDS") facilitate this communication as each individual anchors the scale with their own past experiences. Use the worksheet below to create your own SUDS. For each of the levels on the scale below, think of a time when you felt that degree of distress or anxiety. Since your experience of distress/anxiety may shift as you continue through treatment, it is best to anchor these levels on the scale with specific past events when you felt that way.

100 — 100 = Highest distress/anxiety that you've ever felt or could imagine feeling.
I was at a 100 when...
----

75 — 75 = Marked distress/anxiety: difficult to concentrate on anything else
I was at a 75 when...
----

50 — 50 = Moderate distress/anxiety
I was at a 50 when...
----

25 — 25 = Mild distress/anxiety: easy to shift attention away
I was at a 25 when...
----

0 — 0 = No distress/anxiety; relaxed
I was at a 0 when...

Questions

1. Write down a situation that often triggers your anxiety.

2. What is the worst outcome of this situation?

3. What is the most likely outcome?

4. What is the best outcome?

5. If the worst outcome happens, would it matter a year from now?

Section 4: Facing My Fear

Fear is a natural emotion when someone or something threatens you. Some fears are rational and real, like the fear of fire, while others are only in your head or imagination, like fearing that your classmates will laugh at you if you speak up in class. Since it isn't pleasant, many people think that fear is a negative emotion. However, it can be necessary to protect you from danger. For example, if you are scared of fire, you will never put your hand in it. On the other hand, if your fears are irrational and hold you back in life, they aren't healthy.

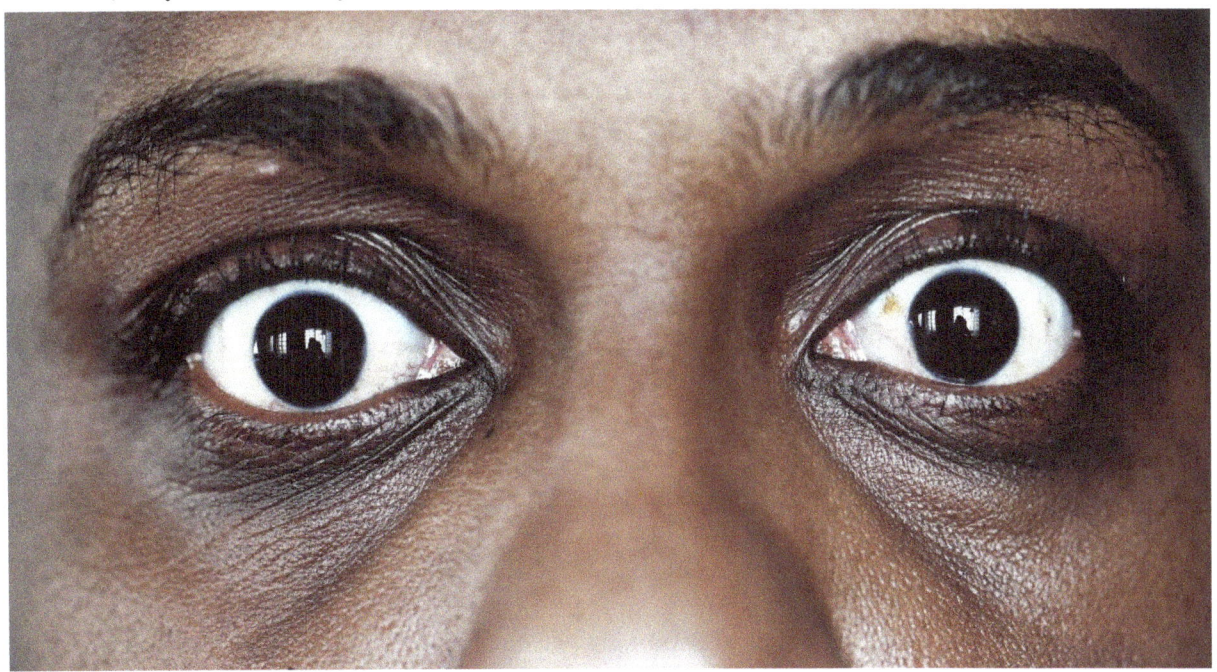

Fears can hold you back.

Fear and phobias can trigger your anxiety and make it hard for you to carry out daily activities.

"Everything you ever wanted is on the other side of fear." George Addair.

Causes of Fear

- Bad childhood memories like getting bitten by a dog or almost drowning
- Dangerous situations that can occur when walking alone at night
- Fear of uncertain situations like fear of the future
- Fears you have learned from the grownups in your life. For example, if your mom is afraid of cats and does not manage that fear around you, she might pass that fear on to you

Symptoms of Fear

- Upset stomach
- Shaking
- Sweating
- Shortness of breath
- Fast heartbeat
- Nausea
- Dry mouth
- Chills
- Chest pain

Fear vs. Worry vs. Phobia

You choose to be worried, but no one chooses fear. Fear is usually based on something real, a natural reaction to danger, while worry is usually in your head, like things you imagine will happen or things that come from your memory. In other words, you make up things in your head to worry about, but fear is out of your control and can be beneficial when it warns you of danger.

A phobia is different from fear and worry because it is an irrational fear of something that isn't dangerous. For example, spiders aren't threatening, yet many people fear them. A phobia is one of the main triggers of anxiety.

Phobia Triggers
- Genetics: if one of your parents has a phobia, you may have one, too
- Learned behavior: if you see your parents afraid of something, you will believe it's scary and develop the same phobia
- Bad experiences with an animal, situation, or place can trigger phobias
- Intense anxiety can also trigger phobias

Worry Triggers
- Unhealthy food
- Technology
- Peer pressure

- Hormonal changes
- Sleep deprivation

An Example of Using CBT to Overcome Fear

Rachel wanted to be an actress, but her stage fright held her back. She thought many times to participate in school plays, but just the thought gave her a stomachache. She tried gradual exposure, where she faced her fear step by step. She started by performing in front of the mirror, then she imagined she was performing in front of an audience. She then began performing in front of her siblings, then friends, then large family members. When she felt comfortable, she started taking small roles in plays until she felt ready to take bigger ones.

Exercises

31. Gradual Exposure

Instructions:

1. Write in this worksheet what your biggest fear is.
2. Starting from the bottom of the ladder, write each step you will take to gradually expose yourself to your fears.
3. The thought of facing your fear may cause you anxiety. It's OK; just take it one step at a time.

For example, if you are afraid of dogs, take these steps:

1. Watch pictures of dogs online.
2. Watch movies with dogs.
3. Be in the same room as a dog with adult supervision, and with the dog on a leash.
4. When you feel comfortable, you can slowly pet the dog while it's still on a leash.
5. When you are ready, remove the leash and play together.

Don't let your fear stop you; push through the anxiety with deep breaths. However, if your feelings are overwhelming or you experience a panic attack, it's time to take a step back and get yourself in a calm mental state. Take your time with each step, and don't move to the next one until you feel comfortable. Reward yourself every time you make progress.

Subjective Units of Distress Scale (SUDS)

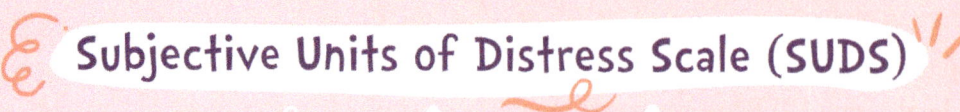

To overcome our fears it can help to build our confidence gradually. You can think of it as being like climbing the steps of a ladder.
Start by writing down the fear that you are facing. Then for each step of the ladder write down one thing you can do to face that fear head-on. Make sure to reward yourself for each step you take

The fear I am facing is: _____

Most difficult

_____
_____
_____
_____
_____
_____
_____
_____
_____
_____
_____
_____

Less difficult

32. Problem-Solving Skills

Instructions:

1. Write in the worksheet one of your fears.
2. Write down all the different ways you can cope with your fear. For example, if you are afraid of talking to new people, you can try taking a few deep breaths beforehand or start making small talk with salespeople.
3. Consider the advantages and disadvantages of each solution and write them down.
4. Choose the best solution and try it.
5. If it doesn't work, find another solution from the list.

You can use this technique with any problem, not just your fears.

PROBLEM SOLVING

 1 Define Your Problem

Before you define a problem, it might feel vague or confusing. Writing out your problem will help to organize information, see it from new angles, and identify the most important issues.

When and where does your problem occur?

What are the causes of your problem?
Think about all the possible causes. Consider your own behavior, as well as external factors.

Define your problem.
Be as clear and comprehensive as possible. If there are many parts to your problem, describe each of them.

> **TIP:** If you find it difficult to separate your emotions from the problem, try to complete this step from the perspective of an impartial friend.

PROBLEM SOLVING

2. Develop Multiple Solutions

Write down at least three solutions to your problem. Without thinking about alternative solutions, we often get stuck on what worked in the past, or the first idea that comes to mind. There are usually many solutions to a problem, and our first ideas aren't always the best.

PROBLEM SOLVING

 **Assess Your Solutions and Choose One**

Begin by throwing out any solutions that are obviously ineffective or impractical. Next, look at your remaining solutions, and determine which ones are the most likely to be successful by examining them in-depth. This can be done by examining the strengths and weaknesses of each solution.

During this stage, you might come up with new solutions, or find that a combination of multiple solutions is better than any one idea.

Solution	Strengths	Weaknesses

TIP: If you're having a hard time thinking of strengths and weaknesses for each solution, ask yourself these questions:

- Is this a short-term or long-term solution?
- How likely am I to follow through with this solution?
- How will this solution affect other people?

PROBLEM SOLVING

 **Implement Your Solution**

To ensure you follow through with your solution, it's best to think of how and when it will be implemented. Without doing so, solutions that are difficult might be avoided, or they can slip your mind when the time comes.

When will you implement your solution?

Some solutions can happen at a specific time (e.g. "2:00 PM on Saturday"), while others require something unpredictable to happen (e.g. "when I get angry"). Fill in the relevant section below:

My solution can be scheduled...

When will you implement your solution? Be specific.

How will you remember to follow through with your solution?

My solution is in response to something...

How will you know when to use your solution?
List specific warning signs, triggers, or other specific events that will tip you off.

List the specific steps you will take to implement your solution.

TIP: If your solution requires a lot of time or effort, try to break the process into small steps. It's easier to follow through with several small steps, rather than one giant task.

PROBLEM SOLVING

5 Review

Finally, after implementing your solution, you will review what worked and what didn't. Even if your problem was a one-time situation, there are often broader lessons to be learned. Take a moment to reflect on your problem and how you handled it.

In what ways was your solution effective?

In what ways was your solution not effective?

If you could go back in time, what would you change about how you handled the problem?

What advice would you give to someone else who was dealing with the same problem?

----

33. Overcoming Safety Behavior

Safety behavior is avoiding your fears to protect yourself. However, this is a temporary solution that can only make your anxiety worse.

Instructions:
1. Ask yourself how often you avoid your fear or anxiety triggers.
2. Write down all the different ways you avoid them, like ordering everything online because making small talk makes you nervous or sitting in the back of the classroom to avoid attention.
3. You can then slowly and gradually do the opposite of each situation, like sitting in the middle of the classroom or ordering food on the phone.
4. Consider the gradual exposure technique, as it helps you make progress at your own pace.

34. Breathing Technique

Instructions:
1. Take a deep and long breath into your abdomen.
2. Breathe out from your mouth.
3. Take another deep breath from your nostrils and notice your belly rising.
4. Close your eyes and imagine the air flowing through your body.
5. Breathe out and release the air from your body.
6. Repeat until you calm down.

35. Art Work

Art is a great way to reduce and cope with fears, worries, and anxiety. Whenever you feel any of these emotions, draw or doodle anything. If you don't like drawing, try coloring books. You can also try other art forms to get you out of your head, like dancing, singing, and writing.

36. Yoga

Yoga is very relaxing and an effective coping skill.

Child's pose.

Iveto, CC BY-SA 4.0 <https://creativecommons.org/licenses/by-sa/4.0>, via Wikimedia Commons: https://commons.wikimedia.org/wiki/File:Balasana.JPG

Instructions:
1. Find a quiet spot at home with no distractions.
2. Sit on the yoga mat, just like the picture.
3. Remain in this position for five minutes.
4. Clear your mind and breathe into your belly.
5. Remain focused, and bring your mind back to the present moment whenever it wanders.

37. Relaxing Meditation

Instructions:
1. Sit in a quiet room in a comfortable position.
2. Close your eyes and take deep and slow breaths.
3. Focus on your breathing and nothing else.
4. If your mind wanders or thoughts creep into your head, don't give them attention and let them pass.

38. Draw Circles

Instructions:
1. Get crayons or pens of different colors and a notebook.
2. Draw circular patterns and keep focused on the drawing activity.
3. The patterns don't have to be pretty; it's the activity that matters.
4. Keep drawing for a few minutes, then change the pattern and the pen or crayon color.

39. Mental Contrasting

Mental contrasting is thinking positively about the future while acknowledging the hardships you might face to reduce your fear of the future.

Instructions:
1. Visualize making your biggest dreams come true or achieving all your goals.
2. Imagine how great your life would be and how you would feel.
3. Acknowledge the problems and hardships that could stand in your way, like lack of motivation.
4. Make a plan to overcome these obstacles.

40. Affirmations

- *I am supported, I am loved, and I am safe.*
- *I am releasing all my fears, worries, and stress.*
- *My mind is quiet and calm.*
- *I am letting go of any emotions that don't serve me.*
- *I treat myself with kindness.*

Section 5: Overcoming Mental Filtering

Mental filtering occurs when you only focus on the negative aspect of a situation and filter out or ignore the positive. In other words, your mind chooses to only see the bad side of life (even if it is small) and refuses to see all the other good things that are happening around you.

For example, you got straight As in all subjects, but you got a C in the last math exam. You only focus on this one exam and tell yourself you are a failure and a bad student. You ignore all the praise you have received from your teachers and all your other good test results and judge yourself based on this one test.

Or your best friend does something to upset you but tries to apologize and make it up to you. However, you don't want to see all their efforts and are only focused on this one mistake.

Mental filtering keeps away the positive thoughts, as a water filter does with dirt, except it filters the good thoughts and leaves you with the bad ones. Understand that there are always good things around you and happy thoughts in your head. Your mind is just keeping them from you,

The Effect of Mental Filtering on Your Life

Mental filtering can help you see the good side of every situation.
https://www.pexels.com/photo/woman-holding-a-smiley-balloon-1236678/

Mental filtering will change the way you view your reality. You will exaggerate the negatives, lower your self-esteem, and have a pessimistic opinion of yourself and the world. You will be blind to all the good things in your life and constantly feel like a failure even if you are accomplished. Eventually, you may fall into depression. Luckily, CBT techniques can do wonders for your thoughts and mental health.

An Example of Using CBT for Mental Filtering

Ryan struggled with seeing the good things in life. He always felt like someone had put a blindfold on his eyes when there was anything good happening around him. However, things started to change when he tried CBT. He used affirmations every day to remind himself that he is an awesome person and that his life is pretty great. The more he repeated words like "I am clever and good at what I do" or "I am lucky to have great family and friends," the more he believed them. So whenever something bad happened, these affirmations quickly challenged these negative thoughts to remind him that one mistake doesn't define him. Eventually, he started to focus more on the positives instead of the negatives.

Exercises

41. ABC Model

This exercise will make you aware of your negative thoughts and mental filtering tendencies so you can change and transform your way of thinking.

Instructions:

1. Write in the "A" in the worksheet an event that has happened recently that triggered negative thoughts.
2. Write in "B" your beliefs or understanding of the event. For example, you are close to one of your classmates, but they didn't invite you to their birthday party, so you believe they don't like you.
3. Write in "C" how the situation made you feel and affected your behavior. For example, you were sad or angry and decided not to talk to your classmate again.
4. In "D," create new beliefs or outcomes to the situation, like maybe they didn't invite you because it was a small party.
5. In "E," come up with new beliefs, like believing that your classmate likes you because they never acted otherwise, and there is probably a misunderstanding.

ABC Model

ACTIVATING EVENT
Something happens to you or in the environment around you.

BELIEFS
You have a belief or interpretation regarding the activating event.

CONSEQUENCES
Your belief has consequences that include feelings and behaviors.

DISPUTATIONS OF BELIEFS
Challenge your beliefs to create new consequences.

EFFECTIVE NEW BELIEFS
Adoption and implementation of new adaptive beliefs.

42. Cognitive Restructuring

This technique can alter your thoughts so you can calmly express your emotions.

- Write down the negative thoughts.
- What evidence do you have that supports it, and what evidence is against it?
- Is this thought based on my emotions or facts?
- Can this thought be more flexible?
- Am I misunderstanding the evidence and just making assumptions?
- If I ask my parents and siblings about this situation, what will their thoughts be?
- Am I ignoring the evidence that doesn't support my thought?
- Am I exaggerating the truth?
- Is my negative thought an automatic response or based on facts?
- Did someone influence my thoughts? Are they trustworthy?
- Is this thought based on something real or a worst-case scenario?

43. Negative Thoughts vs. Positive Thoughts

Fill out the worksheet. This exercise will make you see the difference between your negative and positive thoughts to determine which ones are more rational.

Situation
Something happens. This step covers only the facts of what happened, without any interpretation.

	My Actual Thought	Alternate Thought

Thought
Using thought, you interpret the situation. These interpretations are not always accurate. There are many ways to think about the same situation.

Feeling
You experience emotions based upon your thoughts about the situation.

Behavior
You respond to the situation based upon your thoughts and feelings.

44. Decatastrophizing

Catastrophizing is when you exaggerate a situation in your head and focus on negative outcomes. Decatastrophizing challenges your negative thoughts and gives a realistic view of the situation.

Fill out the worksheet.

Cognitive distortions are irrational thoughts that have the power to influence how you feel. Everyone has some cognitive distortions—they're a normal part of being human. However, when cognitive distortions are too plentiful or extreme, they can be harmful.

One common type of cognitive distortion is called catastrophizing. When catastrophizing, the importance of a problem is exaggerated, or the worst possible outcome is assumed to be true. By learning to question your own thoughts, you can correct many of these cognitive distortions.

What are you worried about?

How likely is it that your worry will come true? Give examples of past experiences, or other evidence, to support your answer.

If your worry does come true, what's the worst that could happen?

If your worry does come true, what's most likely to happen?

If your worry comes true, what are the chances you'll be okay...

In one week? _____%   In one month? _____%   In one year? _____%

45. Thoughts Trial

In this fun exercise, you will pretend one of your negative thoughts is on trial, and you are the judge, prosecutor, and lawyer. Fill out this worksheet and present the evidence that supports it and the evidence against it. After you finish, pass judgment based on the information you provided.

In this exercise, you will put a thought on trial by acting as a defense attorney, prosecutor, and judge, to determine the accuracy of the thought.

Prosecution and Defense:
Gather evidence in support of, and against, your thought. Evidence can only be used if it's a verifiable fact. No interpretations, guesses, or opinions!

Judge:
Come to a verdict regarding your thought. Is the thought accurate and fair? Are there other thoughts that could explain the facts?

THE THOUGHT

THE DEFENSE
evidence for the thought

THE PROSECUTION
evidence against the thought

THE JUDGE'S VERDICT

46. Challenge Your Inner Rules

People have negative or self-critical rules that affect how they see themselves or the world, like "If I fail a test, I am a failure." Fill out the worksheet to better understand your rules.

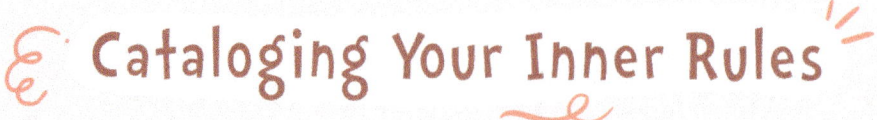

We all have rules that guide our behavior on a daily basis. We might not be able to clearly articulate all of them, but they hang around in our subconscious and nudge us towards behavior that is consistent with them. Many of these rules might be good (e.g., "Good people don't badmouth others behind their back") but some of them might not be adaptive or helpful (e.g., "If you make one mistake, you are a bad person").

Use this worksheet to help you identify a questionable or harmful rule you have and challenge it.

THE INFRACTION

What did you do that broke one of your internal rules?

THE RULE

What rule did your behavior break? Why did you feel bad after engaging in that behavior?

THE RULE'S ORIGINS

Where did it come from? What makes you think the rule is right, or a good rule?

ADVANTAGES OF KEEPING THIS RULE	DISADVANTAGES OF KEEPING THIS RULE
How does this rule help you?	How does this rule hurt you?

What to Do with This Rule: ☐ Keep It   ☐ Trash It   ☐ Modify It

THE RULE GOING FORWARD

What is the best possible version of this rule?

47. Challenge Negative Thoughts

Fill out this worksheet to learn to filter the negative thoughts instead of the positive ones.

48. Role Play

Think of a situation where you filtered positive thoughts. Then, you can mention all the negatives in the situation, and the other person will list the positives. Try to challenge each other with evidence like a lawyer and prosecutor.

49. Affirmations

- *I embrace love and positivity.*
- *I see all the obstacles disappearing from my life.*
- *Today is a good day full of joy and exciting opportunities.*
- *I solve my problems with positive thinking.*
- *I control my thoughts, and I only allow positivity in.*

Section 6: Beating The Blues

Everyone feels sad and even goes through depression at some time in their lives. A person can be laughing and having fun, but inside, they are fighting a battle that no one else knows about. There is no denying that these feelings are hard, and you might feel that no one can understand what you're going through. You aren't alone; sadness, pain, and depression are more common than you think.

Depression can make you feel helpless.
https://www.pexels.com/photo/woman-in-black-jacket-3209136/

In any superhero movie, the hero uses their pain as motivation to keep fighting; they don't allow it to hold them back, and neither should you. Once you understand what you're going through, you can find the right methods and help yourself get better. All the information and exercises in this book can aid in managing depression symptoms and treating the blues.

However, if these techniques don't work, understand that it's OK. There are other ways to get support. Ask a friend, family member, teacher, or someone you trust for help. How many people love you and want to see you feel better will surprise you.

What Is Depression?

Depression is feeling down and blue all the time, accompanied by losing interest in the activities you once enjoyed.

Causes of Depression

- Family history: if someone from your family suffers from depression, there is a possibility you will suffer from it.
- Some personality types are more prone to depression, such as those who suffer from anxiety, low self-esteem, and high sensitivity.
- Being bullied
- Early puberty
- Trauma
- Social media
- Pressure at school

Symptoms of Depression

- Anger
- Loss of energy
- Constantly feeling tired
- Ignoring your appearance and hygiene
- Isolating from family and friends
- Slow movements
- Noticeable weight gain or weight loss
- Sleeping too much or insomnia
- Feeling sad for no reason
- Pessimism or hopelessness
- Irritability
- Feeling guilty or worthless
- Self-criticism or self-blame

CBT is an effective tool for managing sadness and depression because it changes how you think, influencing your behavior and putting you in a good mood. Since sadness and depression are common among teenagers, many have used CBT techniques like thought reframing, meditation, and journaling to challenge their negative thoughts, change their thought patterns, and calm their nerves.

An Example of Someone Using CBT for Anger

Jack used to feel tired all the time and would sleep all day. He was always sad and hopeless, lost his appetite, and suffered anxiety. Jack tried journaling, behavior activation, and thought restructuring to bring his attention to the good things in his life. He also practiced meditation every day to reduce his anxiety.

Exercises

50. Mental Contrast for Depression
Instructions:
1. Imagine your worst-case scenario or fear coming true.
2. Imagine the consequences of this situation.
3. Think about all the tools you can use to prevent this scenario from coming true.
4. Make a plan to use all your resources to prevent it from happening.

51. Pleasant Activity Scheduling (PAS)

Fill this worksheet with the activities and responsibilities that you used to do before the depression to encourage you to go back to your old life. Rate how you feel.

You can begin to decrease depression by engaging in activities you find enjoyable, and by taking care of responsibilities that you have been neglecting.

List three activities you enjoy:

1.
2.
3.

List three responsibilities you need to take care of:

1.
2.
3.

Try doing at least one activity or responsibility each day. Use the following scale to rate your depression, pleasant feelings, and sense of achievement before and after the activity.

```
0    1    2    3    4    5    6    7    8
None                  Moderate              Extreme
```

Activity (location, date, time)		Depression	Pleasure	Achievement
	Before			
	After			
	Before			
	After			
	Before			
	After			

52. Black-and-White Thinking

Black-and-white thinking is believing things are bad or good with no middle ground. This exercise will teach you to let go of this type of thinking.

Black-and-white thinking often uses extreme words like always or never: "I will never succeed" or "I am always failing." Write down ten of your black-and-white thoughts in this worksheet and use words like "I am flexible enough to," "I am willing to," "I am noticing that," or "sometimes."

Black & White Thinking

Black and white thinking, also known as all-or-nothing thinking, is a cognitive distortion that involves seeing things in extreme categories, such as success or failure, good or bad, and right or wrong, without any shades of gray or nuance.

Examples of Black & White Thinking:

"I'm not good enough if I don't get the job."

"If a friend doesn't call me back within an hour, they don't care about me"

"I'm lazy if I don't exercise 5 days a week."

"I can't have both good grades and a social life."

"I'm weak if I can't stick to healthy eating 100% of the time."

Finding the 'Gray' Area:

Write down a black and white thought you had recently, that may not be 100% true all the time, or that is not based 100% on veri able fact. After that, write another perspective that is in the gray area.

Black & White Thought:

If a friend doesn't call me back within an hour, they don't care about me"

Re-framed Thought:

There are many other reasons my friend might not be able to call me back right now, and I don't know for sure if it relates to how much they care.

Black & White Thought:

Re-framed Thought:

Black & White Thinking

Black and white thinking, also known as all-or-nothing thinking, is a cognitive distortion that can cause harm in various aspects of life. It can lead to negative thoughts, self-sabotaging behaviors, and limit opportunities and progress.

How has black and white thinking affected your life?

Fill in the circle for any of the Black and White thinking consequences you have experienced, then write about your experience below.

○ Do my thoughts tend to cause misunderstandings and missed opportunities for compromise and resolution of conflicts in my relationships?

○ Does my fixed mindset prevent me from learning and achieving my full potential?

○ Do my thoughts limit opportunities and hinder collaboration and progress in the workplace?

○ Does my black and white thinking disrupt my healthy eating habits by creating rigid dietary restrictions and unhealthy relationships with food?

○ Do my thoughts lead to negative thoughts and emotions and self-sabotaging behaviors?

○ Do my thoughts cause me to make decisions without considering the impact on myself and others?

○ Do my thoughts lead me to idealize and devalue others, causing emotional upheaval in my relationships?

○ Do my thoughts lead me to make assumptions without verifying facts?

○ Do my thoughts filter out positive information and only focus on the negative?

○ Does my black and white thinking cause anxiety by exaggerating the probability of something negative happening?

How has black and white thinking affected you?

_____
_____
_____
_____

Black & White Thinking

This worksheet will guide you through a series of questions to help you evaluate your thoughts and determine if they involve black and white thinking. Write down a thought you had recently, then check the boxes.

Write down the thought:

_____

_____

_____

YES (May be Black and White Thinking)

- ○ Is the thought overly simplistic or extreme?
- ○ Does the thought involve rigid "should" or "must" statements?
- ○ Does the thought involve thinking in absolutes, such as "always" or "never"?
- ○ Is there no room for nuance or complexity in the thought?
- ○ Does the thought involve jumping to conclusions without considering all the evidence?
- ○ Are there other possible explanations or perspectives that the thought ignores?
- ○ Does the thought involve personalizing or globalizing an event?
- ○ Does the thought involve catastrophizing or minimizing the situation?
- ○ Does the thought involve discounting the positive or exaggerating the negative?
- ○ Does the thought involve focusing on one aspect of the situation and ignoring the others?
- ○ Does the thought involve making assumptions without verifying the facts?
- ○ Does the thought involve overgeneralizing from one negative experience?

Changing black and white thinking takes time to master, but with practice it will become second nature.

53. Overgeneralization

Overgeneralization is applying the same thought to multiple situations. For instance, if you lose one game, you tell yourself, "I never win any games." Try this exercise to challenge these thoughts.

1. Think of someone you love dearly, like your best friend or sibling.
2. Imagine they come to you with one of your overgeneralized thoughts like "I mess up every time I speak in class."
3. Write down three things you would tell them.

- _____

- _____

- _____

4. How different are they from your inner thoughts?
_____

5. Would you tell your sibling the same things you tell yourself? If not, then why not?
_____

6. Why don't you treat yourself with the same kindness?
_____

54. Journaling

1. Write down in your notebook a catastrophizing (exaggerated) thought. This way, you will separate yourself from it and look at it as if it belongs to someone else.
2. When you read it a few times, you will realize that this thought is irrational.
3. You will start to think more objectively and come up with helpful thoughts.

55. Walking Meditation

1. Go for a walk while focusing on each step.
2. Notice how many breaths you take with every step and how fast you walk.
3. Focus on how your lungs feel with every breath.
4. Match your breathing with your steps.
5. Take a deep breath, count three steps, then breathe out and take three steps.
6. Feel the wind in your hair and focus on where you are and what you are doing.

56. Visualization

1. Sit in a quiet room in a comfortable position.
2. Close your eyes and take a few deep breaths.
3. Imagine you are in your favorite place.
4. You can see yourself happy and having fun.
5. Feel everything around you with your five senses to make the image as real as possible.
6. Stay in this place until you feel relaxed.

57. Breathing Exercise

1. Lie down and place one hand on your chest and the other on your stomach.
2. Take a deep breath through your nostrils and let your stomach push your hand out.
3. Breathe out through your lips as if you're whistling.
4. Repeat five times.

58. Label Your Thoughts

1. Close your eyes and take a deep breath.
2. Allow yourself to think of your negative thoughts.
3. Whenever you have a thought, label it as what it is: a "Thought." For example, say, "I am thinking that I am not a good friend."
4. Keep repeating to convince yourself that it's just a thought and not a fact.

59. Affirmations

- *I deserve more than what my mind tells me.*
- *I am enough.*
- *I am a good person.*
- *I find beauty in my broken parts.*
- *My mistakes don't define me.*

Section 7: Controlling Anger

Anger is a strong emotion that you feel when someone insults you or when something goes wrong. When expressed calmly, anger is a helpful feeling that lets others know you are upset or frustrated.

Expressing anger calmly can help people understand that you're frustrated.
https://unsplash.com/photos/sLrw_Cx6u_I?utm_source=unsplash&utm_medium=referral&utm_content=creditShareLink

Anger Triggers

- Feeling misunderstood or unheard
- Getting blamed for something you didn't do
- When someone makes fun of you
- Feeling threatened
- Mistreatment
- Stress

The Effects of Anger on Your Health

- Increases your anxiety
- Depression
- Headaches
- Insomnia
- Skin issues
- Clouds your judgment
- Increases negative thoughts
- Stresses you out
- Isolation
- Low self-esteem
- Violent behavior

CBT will teach you how to control your emotions. These techniques can challenge the negative thoughts caused by anger and replace them with compassionate, helpful, and rational thoughts.

Exercises

60. SUDS Scale

Think of the last time you got angry and rate it from one to ten. Then, color the scale depending on how angry you currently feel. In separate sections, write down the triggers that commonly lead to your anger, and another section to note what you can do to control your anger effectively.

61. Cognitive Restructuring

Cognitive restructuring or cognitive reframing is a CBT method that makes you notice your negative thoughts and challenge them. You will eventually realize that these thoughts are either irrational or exaggerated in your head. You can then "reframe" them to start thinking positively.

Fill the worksheet just like in exercise number 43, but focus on thoughts that made you angry.

- Write down the negative thought.
- What evidence do you have that supports it, and what evidence is against it?

- Is this thought based on my emotions or facts?
- Can this thought be more flexible?
- Am I misunderstanding the evidence and just making assumptions?
- If I ask my parents and siblings about this situation, what will their thoughts be?
- Am I ignoring the evidence that doesn't support my thought?
- Am I exaggerating the truth?
- Is my negative thought an automatic response or based on facts?
- Did someone influence my thoughts? Are they trustworthy?
- Is this thought based on something real or a worst-case scenario?

62. Behavioral Experiment

Anger is usually based on irrational thoughts that intensify your emotions and make you lose your temper. This exercise will test the negative thoughts to see how they affect your behavior and mood. Just imagine a scenario with this thought and predict how you will react. Or you can experiment with it by thinking about this thought with your family and friends and seeing its effect on you.

Behavioral Experiment

Our thoughts and beliefs determine how we feel, and how we act, at any given moment. Even thoughts that are irrational impact our mood and behavior, often negatively. A behavioral experiment is a tool for testing our thoughts and beliefs, and replacing those that are irrational with healthy alternatives.

Part 1: Experiment Plan

Thought to Test
What is the thought or belief you would like to test?

Experiment
How can you test this thought?

When will you run the experiment?

Prediction
What do you think will happen during the experiment?

How do you expect to feel after the experiment?

VERY BAD — NEUTRAL — VERY GOOD

Part 2: Experiment Results

Outcome
What happened during the experiment?

How did you feel after the experiment?

VERY BAD — NEUTRAL — VERY GOOD

New Thought
Given the evidence from the experiment, what is your new thought?

----

63. Track Your Mood

Use this worksheet to track your mood for a week to identify negative thoughts.

Weekly Mood Chart

	Monday	Tuesday	Wednesday	Thursday	Friday	Saturday	Sunday
6 AM - 10 AM							
10 AM - 2 PM							
2 PM - 6 PM							
6 PM - 10 PM							
10 PM - 2 AM							
2 AM - 6 AM							

64. Daily Mood Chart

This exercise will track your emotions every day so you can monitor your angry behavior.

	Happy	Sad	Mad	Tired	Excited	Anxious	Other	Notes
6 AM - 8 AM								
8 AM - 10 AM								
10 AM - 12 PM								
12 PM - 2 PM								
2 PM - 4 PM								
4 PM - 6 PM								
6 PM - 8 PM								
8 PM - 10 PM								
10 PM - 12 AM								
12 AM - 2 AM								
2 AM - 4 AM								
4 AM - 6 AM								

65. Thought Log

Write an event that angered you, your negative thoughts, how they affected your behavior and actions, and how you wish you responded.

Event	Thought	Consequence (emotion & behavior)	Alternate Response

66. Anger Diary

Every night before you go to sleep, reflect on a person or situation that made you angry.

Anger Diary

EXAMPLE		
	Trigger	
	Warning Signs	
	Anger Response	
	Outcome	

EVENT ONE		
	Trigger	
	Warning Signs	
	Anger Response	
	Outcome	

EVENT TWO		
	Trigger	
	Warning Signs	
	Anger Response	
	Outcome	

 Anger Diary

EVENT THREE

Trigger	
Warning Signs	
Anger Response	
Outcome	

EVENT FOUR

Trigger	
Warning Signs	
Anger Response	
Outcome	

EVENT FIVE

Trigger	
Warning Signs	
Anger Response	
Outcome	

REVIEW

Do you notice any patterns related to your anger?	
Generally, how would you like to react differently?	

67. Meditation
Instructions:
1. Take a deep breath and focus on your feet.
2. Flex, move your toes, and imagine the anger leaving your body through your toes.
3. Next, focus on your legs and squeeze the muscles, then imagine the anger leaving your body from your legs.
4. Repeat the previous steps with your torso, neck, shoulders, arms, and face.

68. Breathing Exercise
Instructions:
1. Hold a flower and take a deep breath, taking in its scent.
2. Hold your breath while counting to three.
3. Breathe out through your mouth and count to four.
4. Repeat until you calm down.

69. Affirmations
- *I am in control of my anger.*
- *I choose to respond with kindness rather than anger.*
- *My heart and mind are free of anger and anxiety.*
- *I will never choose anger.*
- *I express myself with understanding and respect.*

Section 8: My Self-Esteem

Self-esteem is how you see and value yourself. It's your self-beliefs and your opinions about your looks, personality, character, and life. Low self-esteem is common among many teenagers who often question their identity and if they are good enough and compare themselves to their peers.

Being bullied can affect your self-esteem.
https://www.pexels.com/photo/a-student-getting-bullied-by-schoolmates-7396383/

Factors Influencing Your Self-Esteem

How many hours do you spend on social media? Your parents have probably told you many times to put the phone down, but you just can't. However, they have a point here. Social media can damage your self-esteem.

All the pictures you see online are either filtered or heavily edited. The "spontaneous" photos your favorite celebrities post of themselves are anything but spontaneous. It takes them hours to get the right lighting, makeup, and pose to make it look like it does. Even the "no makeup look" is a lie. No one posts a picture of themselves showing the dark lines under their eyes. They actually use makeup that looks natural. All these images can lower your self-esteem as you keep comparing yourself to these unrealistic beauty standards.

You also see people online posting about their vacations and having fun, and you feel your life is boring in comparison. Understand that nothing you see on social media is real. People only post about the good things in their lives. No one will post about crying themselves to sleep or having a broken heart.

Loneliness can also affect your self-esteem. Spending time alone with your negative thoughts can make you feel bad about yourself. You should be around people who lift you up and make you happy!

Exercises

70. Challenge the Thought

Whenever you have a negative thought that affects your self-esteem, ask yourself, "What is this thought costing me?"

71. Name Your Inner Critic

Giving your inner critic a name will distance you from them so you can look at these thoughts objectively.

Inner Critic Worksheet

Name:

Date:

The Inner Critic is the Voice of Self Doubt

Ways to Recognize Your Inner Critic:

1. Voice critiques you harshly.

2. You feel out of control of this voice. More like you hear it then you create it.

3. It repeats itself over and over (broken record).

4. You know the thought is untrue but it doesn't leave you.

5. It attacks you for hosting the thoughts it just put in your head ie: "Don't be so insecure."

6. It has black and white thinking.

7. It makes arguments that are in your best interest to keep you safe. It often echoes people in your life who are outer critics.

8. It tells us that we are not ready yet (Need to do more work, need for education).

9. It tells us what we are not good at (ie: "You are not good at numbers, technology or public speaking").

1. Getting to Know Your Inner Critic

• What does your critic say?
Write down some of your inner critic's most frequently voiced beliefs.

 Inner Critic Worksheet

- Who from your current life or past does the inner critic echo or build upon when it speaks?
Family members, old teachers, cultural messages?

- How would you describe your inner critic? Anxious? People-pleasing? Persistent? Pick five words the describe it.

------

2. Create Your Character

Inner Critic Worksheet

3. Name your Character:

....

....

....

....

Ways to Distinguish Inner Critic From Realistic Thinking

Inner Critic	Realistic Thinking
Definite pronouncements	Curious questions
Black and White	Able to see the gray
Repetitive	Forward-thinking
Emotionally charged	Emotionally grounded
No interest in actual evidence	Interested in gathering info
Retreat	Explore
Focus on problems/lacking areas	Seeks solutions
Anxious tone	Calmer tone
Self-critique	Self-care

Inner Critic Worksheet

Ways to Work with Your Inner Critic

1. Naming   label and notice

2. Removing from the scene

3. Compassionate understanding of the critic's motives

4. Thanks, but no thanks

5. Separate the I from the Inner Critic

6. Create a character that personifies your inner critic

7. Humor

8. Turn down the volume

9. Move the voice (picture the voice receding into space)

10. Thanks but I got this one covered. *******

72. Recognize Thought Distortion

Challenge the thoughts that affect your self-esteem with this exercise.

Thought Distortion Monitoring Record

Situation Who were you with? What were you doing? Where were you? When did it happen?	Automatic thought What went through your mind? (Thoughts, images, or memories)	Emotions & body sensations What did you feel? (Rate intensity 0 - 100%)	Unhelpful thinking style Does your thought fall in to any of these common traps?
			☐ **ALL OR NOTHING THINKING** Thinking in extremes. For example, something is either 100% good or bad ☐ **CATASTROPHIZING** Jumping to the worst possible conclusion ☐ **OVER GENERALIZING** Seeing a pattern based upon a single event ☐ **MENTAL FILTER** Only paying attention to certain types of evidence ("that doesn't count") ☐ **DISQUALIFYING THE POSITIVE** Discounting positive information or twisting a positive into a negative ☐ **JUMPING TO CONCLUSIONS** Mind reading or predicting the future ☐ **MINIMIZATION** Discounting the importance of something ☐ **EMOTIONAL REASONING** Assuming that because we feel a certain way our hunch must be true ☐ **DEMANDS** Using words like 'should', 'must', and 'ought' ☐ **LABELLING** Assigning labels to ourselves or others ("I'm rubbish") ☐ **PERSONALIZATION** Taking too much or too little responsibility ☐ **LOW FRUSTRATION TOLERANCE** Saying things like "this is too difficult", "this is unbearable" or "I can't stand it"

73. Love Letter

Write a love letter to yourself.

Love Letter

74. Remind Yourself of Your Strengths

Remind yourself of how awesome you are by filling out this worksheet.

My Strengths and Qualities

Things I am good at...
1.
2.
3.

Compliments I have received...
1.
2.
3.

What I like about my appearance...
1.
2.
3.

Challenges I have overcome...
1.
2.
3.

I have helped others by...
1.
2.
3.

Things that make me unique...
1.
2.
3.

What I value the most...
1.
2.
3.

Times I have made others happy...
1.
2.
3.

75. Story of Your Life
Write three stories about yourself by following the instructions in the worksheet.

LIFE STORY
The Past, Present, and Future

Writing a story about your life can help you find meaning and value in your experiences. It will allow you to organize your thoughts and use them to grow. People who develop stories about their life tend to experience a greater sense of meaning, which can contribute to happiness.

The Past
Write the story of your past. Be sure to describe challenges you've overcome, and the personal strengths that allowed you to do so.

LIFE STORY

The Past, Present, and Future

The Present

Describe your life and who you are now. How do you differ from your past self? What are your strengths now? What challenges are you facing?

LIFE STORY

The Past, Present, and Future

The Future
Write about your ideal future. How will your life be different than it is now? How will you be different than you are now?

76. Gratitude Journal

Remind yourself of all the amazing things you have in your life by writing three things you are grateful for every day.

GRATITUDE JOURNAL
Three Good Things

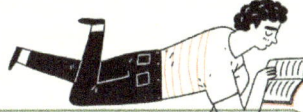

DAY 1

One good thing that happened to me today...

Something good that I saw someone do...

Today I had fun when...

DAY 2

Something I accomplished today...

Something funny that happened today...

Someone I was thankful for today...

GRATITUDE JOURNAL

Three Good Things

DAY 3

Something I was thankful for today...

Today I smiled when...

Something about today I'll always want to remember...

DAY 4

One good thing that happened to me today...

Today was special because...

Today I was proud of myself because...

GRATITUDE JOURNAL

Three Good Things

DAY 5

Something interesting that happened today...

Someone I was thankful for today...

Today I had fun when...

DAY 6

Something about today I'll always want to remember...

Something funny that happened today...

My favorite part of today...

GRATITUDE JOURNAL

Three Good Things

DAY 7

Something I was happy about today...

Something good I saw someone do today...

Something I did well today...

77. Set Life-Enhancing Goals

Set weekly goals to improve your life, like exercising, studying harder, spending less time on social media, or eating healthy.

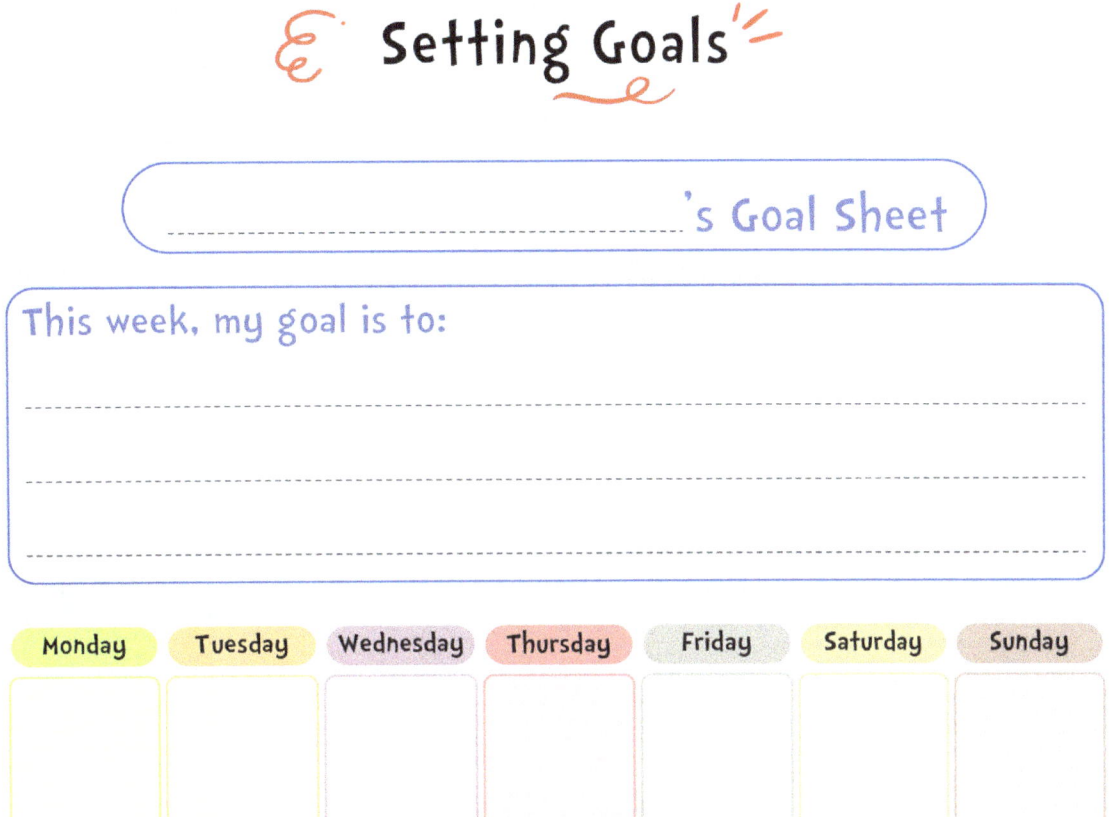

78. Forgive Yourself

Forgive yourself for all your past mistakes and things you feel guilty about that are affecting your self-esteem. Write down the things you blame yourself for; take time to forgive yourself for each one, promising never to think about them again.

79. Affirmations

- *I celebrate my uniqueness.*
- *I am beautiful on the inside and outside.*
- *I am perfect and will continue improving and growing.*
- *I accept every part of me.*
- *I am becoming the best version of myself.*

Section 9: No More "Shoulds"

Societal expectations, peer pressure, and rules you force on yourself shape your thoughts, choices, and behaviors. Most of the time, you do what you "should" rather than what you want to do.

Peer pressure may force you to change your behavior.
https://unsplash.com/photos/QozzJpFZ2lg?utm_source=unsplash&utm_medium=referral&utm_content=creditShareLink

"Should" statements are strict rules that dictate how you should behave, act, and live. These thoughts put you under a lot of pressure as you feel you must act in a certain way. You will feel guilty and ashamed if you fail to follow these rules. You have probably caught yourself saying, "I should work out more" or "I should lose weight."

"Should" statements change how you think and become a part of your identity. You don't often realize the effect these thoughts have. When you put unreasonable and unrealistic demands on yourself, you will feel anxious, angry, and sad and will struggle to achieve your goals.

Exercises

80. Why?

"Should" statements have become your natural reaction, so much so that you don't even think about them. Challenge these thoughts by asking, "Why?" This will lead you to explore and identify their authentic values. In other words, you will discover if these thoughts make any difference in your life or if you are just following these rules because you "Should."

Should Statements

Why

Do you need these thoughts in your life?

81. Set Realistic Goals

After identifying the "Should" rules that match your values, change them to goals to relieve the pressure off yourself. For example, turn "I should lose weight" to "My goal is to lose weight and be healthy."

Should Statements/Values

_____

_____

_____

_____

My Goals

_____

_____

_____

_____

82. Rephrase Should Statements

Rephrasing "Should" statements changes how you feel about these thoughts and won't make you feel guilty if you can't achieve them. For example, turn "I shouldn't spend so much time on social media" to "I would like to spend less time on social media."

Should Statements

New Thoughts

83. Remove "Should"

Remove the word "Should" from the thought to get to the root of your true feelings. For instance, "I shouldn't feel hurt by what they said" will become "I feel hurt by what they said." See the difference?

Statements With Should

Statements Without Should

84. Explore Your Feelings

You may struggle with letting go of "Should" statements. So explore how they make you feel to understand their effect on your mental and emotional health.

Should Statements

_____

_____

_____

How They Make Me Feel

_____

_____

_____

85. Repeat the Thoughts

Write down the "Should" statements, then stand in front of a mirror and repeat them to yourself using "You" instead of "I" or "me." You will realize how damaging these statements are to your self-esteem and that you have been hard on yourself.

86. Meditation

Instructions:

1. Stand under the shower and set the water to a warm temperature.
2. Choose a shower gel scent that relaxes your senses.
3. Feel the water on your skin and every part of your body.
4. Whenever you have an intrusive thought, visualize it going down the drain.
5. Only focus on the present moment and what you are doing, and allow yourself to relax.

87. 4-7-8 Breathing Exercise

Instructions:
1. Place the tip of your tongue behind your upper teeth.
2. Breathe out through your mouth and make a "whoosh" sound.
3. Close your mouth and take a deep breath through your nostrils while counting to four.
4. Hold your breath while counting to seven.
5. Breathe out through your mouth while counting to eight.

88. Write a Letter to Your Future Self

Write a letter to your future self, expressing your life when you lived by "Should" statements and what you hope it will be like when you abandon these thoughts. Read this letter whenever these thoughts creep into your head.

89. Affirmations

- *I live by my own values.*
- *I won't let anyone dictate my thoughts.*
- *I choose a life that makes me happy.*
- *I won't let society's rules influence my thoughts.*
- *I am free to live my life by my own rules.*

Section 10: Peace Within You

It is believed that each person has inner peace. A lot of noise around you can stress you out or cause you anxiety. You need to find your inner peace and use it to silence the negative thoughts in your head.

Finding your inner peace can quiet the negative thoughts in your head.
https://unsplash.com/photos/long-exposure-photography-of-trees-1XGlbRjt92Q

Benefits of Inner Peace and Emotional Balance

- Reduces your stress
- Makes you appreciate the present and be happy
- You avoid bad habits
- You focus on your goals
- Improves your focus
- Gives you power and inner strength
- The ability to recover from setbacks
- Having strong relationships

Mindfulness

You can achieve inner peace by practicing mindful exercises like meditation or breathing exercises. Mindfulness is being present in the here and now and fully aware of your surroundings, your emotions, and what you are doing. This ability protects you from being overwhelmed in any situation and teaches you to react calmly rather than being overwhelmed by your emotions. It is an effective tool against stress and anxiety.

Exercises

90. Reflection Questions

Think hard before answering these questions.

1. If you could change one thing about your life, what would it be and why?

2. If you had the power to travel to the future, ask yourself one question: where/when would it be and why?

3. Think back to the time when you were happiest; what made these days special and why?

___

___

___

91. Mindful Breathing
Instructions:
1. Spread your fingers so your hand looks like a star.
2. Slowly trace your hand's outline using your other hand's pointer finger.
3. Take a deep breath while tracing up from your wrist's tip to your thumb's tip.
4. Breathe out while tracing down the other side of your thumb.
5. Repeat one more time on the same hand and then twice on the other.

92. Mindful Breathing #2
Instructions:
1. Spread out your palm and imagine your hand is a birthday cake and each finger is a candle.
2. Take a deep breath and slowly exhale to blow out each candle.
3. Lower your fingers when you are done, then repeat on the other hand.

93. Body Scan
Instructions:
1. Lie down and close your eyes.
2. Take slow and deep breaths from your belly.
3. Next, bring your attention to your feet and notice how it feels.
4. Notice if you experience any thoughts or emotions, and breathe through them.
5. If you experience any uncomfortable sensation, breathe into it and notice if it changes.
6. Visualize the tension releasing from your body and then disappearing.
7. Repeat with every part of your body.

94. Self-Care Techniques
- Sleep well
- Eat healthily
- Stay hydrated
- Avoid stress and its triggers
- Relax by doing something you enjoy, like watching TV or listening to music
- Get active by dancing and going for walks
- Limit the time you spend on social media

- Get out of the house and spend time with your friends
- Get creative by drawing or writing
- Treat yourself by eating a nice meal or dessert

95. Mindful Eating
Instructions:
1. Grab a piece of your favorite fruit or vegetable.
2. Plan to eat the food while only focusing on the activity of eating and nothing else.
3. Observe the food's shape and color, and notice how it feels in your hand.
4. Take a bite and notice how your mouth moves.
5. Pay attention to the flavor and describe it to yourself.
6. Swallow and feel the aftertaste.
7. Repeat until you finish eating.

96. Yoga
Practice the yoga pose in this illustration and remain in this position for a couple of minutes.

97. Mindful Stretching
Practice the side-to-side neck stretch by pulling your head with one hand from each side, like in the illustration.

98. Connect to Your Senses
Instructions:
1. Look around the room and name five objects you see.
2. Then, name four objects you can touch.
3. Name three sounds you can hear.
4. Name two scents you can smell.
5. Finally, name one thing you can taste.

99. Affirmations
- *I am at peace with the person I have become.*
- *I am surrounded by harmony and peace.*
- *I am connecting to my inner peace.*
- *Peace follows me wherever I go.*
- *Every part of me attracts joy and peace.*

Mindfulness Tracking Sheet

Practice Log

Instruction: Each time you do a formal throughout the weeks of this program, fill out the following log. As you fill it out, and as you look back over the previous week's practice, think about how your practice has been going. Do you notice any patterns about what works best for you? What changes could you make to sustain the discipline? There is an example to show you how to do this.

Date and Formal Practice	Time	Informal Practice	Thoughts, feelings, and sensations that arose during practice and how you felt afterward
12/21 Breathing Space	8 a.m.	Brushing Teeth	My mind kept wandering to all the work I had to do today. I noticed a tightening in my chest at times, but it subsided. That tightness in my chest was anxiousness, and I felt more calm after the practice. For the informal, I never really noticed the sensations of the bristles on my gums, interesting.

Mindfulness Tracking Sheet

Date and Formal Practice	Time	Informal Practice	Thoughts, feelings, and sensations that arose during practice and how you felt afterward

Bonus Section: My Behavior Log

Activity 101

Record in this worksheet all the times you felt anxious during the day, and answer the questions at the end. Print this log to keep track of your anxiety for as long as you need.

 # THOUGHT RECORD

A thought record is helpful for keeping track of your anxiety thoughts throughout the week. Whenever those thoughts come up, make sure to write them down here. Make an effort to change your anxiety thoughts into positive ones and see what happens!

What happened? (Trigger)	How did it make me feel?	Anxiety thoughts that I had	New positive thoughts I tried	What happened? (Outcome)

Then, answer these questions.
1. Does making a behavioral log make you more or less anxious? Why?
2. What was it like to pay attention to your feelings of anxiety by keeping this log?
3. Were you aware that you had many anxiety-related thoughts?
4. What do you want to do to overcome your anxiety?

Thank You

You did it! You finished the book and took a real and powerful step to improve your life. There is no denying that being a teenager has its challenges, but you made the healthy choice to equip yourself with the right tools to get through this stage.

Anxiety, anger, negative thoughts, and fears aren't easy to live with. They can seriously affect your mood, personality, and well-being. CBT can transform your life and put you in control of your emotions rather than have them control you. You will be impressed with how you react to different situations and your ability to handle them.

Thank you for trusting this book and going on this journey!

Check out another book in the series

References

(ma), V. S., & (PhD), C. D. (2023, May 14). Mental filtering: Definition and examples. Helpful Professor. https://helpfulprofessor.com/mental-filtering/

(N.d.-a). Org.uk. https://www.mind.org.uk/information-support/drugs-and-treatments/talking-therapy-and-counselling/cognitive-behavioural-therapy-cbt/

(N.d.-b). Choosingtherapy.com. https://www.choosingtherapy.com/cbt-kids-teens/

(N.d.-c). Iscainfo.com. https://iscainfo.com/resources/Documents/CBT%20for%20Teens.pdf

(N.d.-d). Washington.edu. https://depts.washington.edu/uwhatc/wp-content/uploads/2022/07/Cognitive-Triangle_Worksheet_Coping_and_Processing.pdf

(N.d.-e). Therapistaid.com. https://www.therapistaid.com/worksheets/automatic-thoughts

(N.d.-f). Org.uk. https://www.mind.org.uk/information-support/types-of-mental-health-problems/anxiety-and-panic-attacks/causes/

(N.d.-g). Choosingtherapy.com. https://www.choosingtherapy.com/cbt-for-anxiety/

(N.d.-h). Therapistaid.com. https://www.therapistaid.com/worksheets/abc-model-for-rebt

(N.d.-i). Org.uk. https://www.mind.org.uk/information-support/types-of-mental-health-problems/anger/causes-of-anger/

(N.d.-j). Choosingtherapy.com. https://www.choosingtherapy.com/cbt-for-anger/#:~:text=CBT%20for%20anger%20can%20assist,rational%2C%20self%2Dcompassionate%20thoughts.

(N.d.-k). Therapistaid.com. https://www.therapistaid.com/worksheets/behavioral-experiment

(N.d.-l). Therapistaid.com. https://www.therapistaid.com/worksheets/anger-diary

(N.d.-m). Psycom.net. https://www.psycom.net/depression-test

(N.d.-n). Choosingtherapy.com. https://www.choosingtherapy.com/cbt-for-depression/

(N.d.-o). Org.uk. https://www.mind.org.uk/information-support/types-of-mental-health-problems/self-esteem/about-self-esteem/

15 core CBT techniques you can use right now. (2019, July 9). Mark Tyrrell's Therapy Skills; Mark Tyrrell. https://www.unk.com/blog/15-core-cbt-techniques-you-can-use-right-now/

3 instantly calming CBT techniques for anxiety. (2016, March 8). Mark Tyrrell's Therapy Skills; Mark Tyrrell. https://www.unk.com/blog/3-instantly-calming-cbt-techniques-for-anxiety/

50 ways to start practicing self-care. (2016, July 21). International Bipolar Foundation. https://ibpf.org/articles/50-ways-to-start-practicing-self-care/

99 self-love affirmations to use when you're feeling insecure & self-critical. (2023, February 20). Mindbodygreen. https://www.mindbodygreen.com/articles/self-love-affirmations

Albert Bonfil, P. (2022, August 12). Cognitive distortions: Overgeneralizing –. Cognitive Behavioral Therapy Los Angeles. https://cogbtherapy.com/cbt-blog/cognitive-distortions-overgeneralizing

Andrews, W. (2021, May 10). Unhealthy thinking patterns: Should statements ». Design.org. https://design.org/unhealthy-thinking-patterns-should-statements/

Anger - how it affects people. (n.d.). Gov.au. https://www.betterhealth.vic.gov.au/health/healthyliving/anger-how-it-affects-people

Ankrom, S. (2008, June 15). 9 breathing exercises to relieve anxiety. Verywell Mind. https://www.verywellmind.com/abdominal-breathing-2584115

Anxiety disorders. (2018, May 4). Mayo Clinic. https://www.mayoclinic.org/diseases-conditions/anxiety/symptoms-causes/syc-20350961

Anxiety disorders. (n.d.). Cleveland Clinic. https://my.clevelandclinic.org/health/diseases/9536-anxiety-disorders

Arlin Cuncic, M. A. (2010, August 31). What Is Overgeneralization? Verywell Mind. https://www.verywellmind.com/overgeneralization-3024614

Automatic thoughts. (n.d.). Therapist Aid. https://www.therapistaid.com/therapy-worksheet/automatic-thoughts

Behavioral experiment. (n.d.). Therapist Aid. https://www.therapistaid.com/therapy-worksheet/behavioral-experiment/cbt/none

Brady, K. (2020, August 19). 5 ways to stop catastrophizing. Keir Brady Counseling Services. https://keirbradycounseling.com/catastrophizing/

Breathing exercises (deep breathing) to reduce anxiety & depression. (n.d.). https://restorativestrength.com/breathing-exercises-for-anxiety-and-depression/

By, P. (n.d.). List of Emotions. Therapistaid.com. https://www.therapistaid.com/worksheets/list-of-emotions

Carol. (2022, April 30). Mental filtering: What to know about this cognitive distortion. A Cognitive Connection. https://acognitiveconnection.com/cognitive-distortion-mental-filtering/

Casabianca, S. S., & Shatzman, C. (2022, April 25). Positive affirmations for anxiety: Reframing your worry to calm down. Psych Central. https://psychcentral.com/anxiety/affirmations-for-anxiety

CCPS. (2015, February 16). 7 benefits of Cognitive Behavioral Therapy. Comprehensive Consultation Psychological Services. https://comprehendthemind.com/7-benefits-cognitive-behavioral-therapy/

Challenging anxious thoughts. (n.d.). Therapistaid.com. https://www.therapistaid.com/worksheets/challenging-anxious-thoughts

Clinic, A. R. (2020, October 26). The goals of cognitive behavioral therapy? Aquila Recovery Clinic; Aquila Recovery. https://www.aquilarecovery.com/blog/what-are-the-goals-of-cognitive-behavioral-therapy/

Coffey, C. (2018, October 2). 30 Affirmations To Stop Comparing And Celebrate You. Thecoffeybreak.com. https://www.thecoffeybreak.com/blog-2/2018/10/2/30-affirmations-to-stop-comparing-and-celebrate-you

Cognitive restructuring: Decatastrophizing. (n.d.). Therapist Aid. https://www.therapistaid.com/therapy-worksheet/decatastrophizing/cbt/none

Content, M. (n.d.). Journaling: Using 4 Cognitive behavioural therapy exercises. Mossery.

Core beliefs info sheet. (n.d.). Therapist Aid. https://www.therapistaid.com/therapy-worksheet/core-beliefs-info-sheet/cbt/adolescents

Counselling Matters. (2020, October 12). Anger management-understanding triggers–. Counselling Matters. https://counselling-matters.org.uk/anger-management-understanding-triggers/

Courtney E. Ackerman, M. A. (2017a, March 20). CBT techniques: 25 cognitive behavioral therapy worksheets. Positivepsychology.com. https://positivepsychology.com/cbt-cognitive-behavioral-therapy-techniques-worksheets/

Courtney E. Ackerman, M. A. (2017b, September 29). Cognitive distortions: 22 examples & worksheets (& PDF). Positivepsychology.com. https://positivepsychology.com/cognitive-distortions/

Courtney E. Ackerman, M. A. (2018, July 12). What is self-acceptance? 25 exercises + definition & quotes. Positivepsychology.com. https://positivepsychology.com/self-acceptance/

Cundiff, D. (2022, December 19). Benefits of cognitive behavioral therapy. Bayview Recovery Rehab Center. https://www.bayviewrecovery.com/rehab-blog/5-benefits-of-cognitive-behavioral-therapy/

Decatastrophizing. (2023, February 21). Psychology Tools. https://www.psychologytools.com/resource/decatastrophizing/

Department of Health, & Human Services. (n.d.). Depression explained. Gov.au. https://www.betterhealth.vic.gov.au/health/conditionsandtreatments/depression

Deschene, L. (2020, May 14). 8 quick and easy meditation techniques to calm your anxious mind. Tiny Buddha. https://tinybuddha.com/blog/mindfulness-peace-blog/8-quick-and-easy-meditation-techniques-to-calm-your-anxious-mind/

Distinguish between fear and worry. (n.d.). Gdba.com. https://gdba.com/distinguish-between-fear-and-worry/

Driscoll, L. (2020, September 20). 7 CBT activities you can use in school counseling. Social Emotional Workshop. https://www.socialemotionalworkshop.com/cbt-activities-school-counseling/

Dysfunctional Thought Record. (n.d.). B-cdn.net. https://positive.b-cdn.net/wp-content/uploads/2017/06/Dysfunctional-Thought-Record.pdf

Elizabeth, D. (2022, August 4). 53 affirmations for rest and relaxation. Wild Simple Joy. https://wildsimplejoy.com/affirmations-for-rest-and-relaxation/

Emma McAdam, L. (2021, May 22). Mental Filtering: Thinking this way might make you depressed. Therapy in a Nutshell. https://therapyinanutshell.com/mental-filtering/

Emotional balance –. (n.d.). Alternative Health Care Center. http://www.alternativehealthcaredoc.com/emotional-balance

Eskin, C. K. (2021, December 22). Why teens don't talk to their parents. Teen Line. https://www.teenline.org/post/why-teens-don-t-talk-to-their-parents

Example Sheet. (n.d.). The Cognitive Model. Therapistaid.com. https://www.therapistaid.com/worksheets/cognitive-model-example-practice

Facing Your Fears (CYP). (2023, February 21). Psychology Tools. https://www.psychologytools.com/resource/facing-your-fears-cyp/

Felman, A. (2020, January 11). Anxiety: Symptoms, types, causes, prevention, and treatment. Medicalnewstoday.com. https://www.medicalnewstoday.com/articles/323454

Find your inner peace: techniques and benefits. (n.d.). Beaire.com. https://beaire.com/en/aire-magazine/find-your-inner-peace

Fritscher, L. (2008, March 15). The psychology of fear. Verywell Mind. https://www.verywellmind.com/the-psychology-of-fear-2671696

Gillette, H. (2010, March 4). Why are teens depressed? 6 reasons. Psych Central. https://psychcentral.com/depression/why-are-so-many-teens-depressed

GoodRx - error. (n.d.). Goodrx.com. https://www.goodrx.com/health-topic/mental-health/fear-vs-phobia

Gower, B. S., & Stokes, M. C. (Eds.). (2020). Socratic Questions: New Essays on the Philosophy of Socrates and its Significance. Routledge.

Hadiah. (2023, June 12). Top 10 practical CBT exercises for anxiety relief (+FREE worksheets PDF). Ineffable Living; Hadiah. https://ineffableliving.com/treat-your-anxiety-using-cognitive-behavioral-therapy-cbt/

Harrison, P. (2018, February 18). 19 mindfulness-Based Cognitive Behavioral Therapy exercises [CBT]. The Daily Meditation Coaching Sessions; The Daily Meditation. https://www.thedailymeditation.com/cbt-exercises

Harrison, P. (2019, August 22). 4 mindful eating meditation scripts you need to try. The Daily Meditation Coaching Sessions; The Daily Meditation. https://www.thedailymeditation.com/mindful-eating-3

Holland, K., & Nave, K. (2013, December 9). Cognitive behavioral therapy for depression. Healthline. https://www.healthline.com/health/depression/cognitive-behavioral-therapy

Holy, L. (2021, March 1). 10 yoga poses for relaxation & calming. Banyanbotanicals.com; Banyan Botanicals. https://www.banyanbotanicals.com/info/blog-the-banyan-insight/details/10-yoga-poses-for-relaxation-anxiety/

How I Feel. (n.d.). Therapist Aid. https://www.therapistaid.com/therapy-worksheet/how-i-feel-cbt-tool/cbt/adolescents

Kapoor, A. (2021, July 27). How to do Body Scan Meditation and its benefits. Calm Sage. https://www.calmsage.com/mindfulness-body-scan-meditation/

Kendra Cherry, M. (2009, March 3). What is cognitive behavioral therapy (CBT)? Verywell Mind. https://www.verywellmind.com/what-is-cognitive-behavior-therapy-2795747

Kendra Cherry, M. (2013, August 2). Emotions and types of emotional responses. Verywell Mind. https://www.verywellmind.com/what-are-emotions-2795178

Kristenson, S. (2022, April 12). 60 calming affirmations for managing your anger. Happier Human; Steve Scott. https://www.happierhuman.com/affirmations-anger/

Kristenson, S. (2023, July 10). 60 affirmations for a calming peace of mind. Happier Human; Steve Scott. https://www.happierhuman.com/affirmations-peace/

LaBarbara, S. (2022, August 25). The trouble with 'should statements' and how to reframe them. A Good Place. https://www.agoodplacetherapy.com/the-blog/should-statements

Lamoreux, K. (2016, January 24). 1-minute mindfulness exercises. Psych Central. https://psychcentral.com/health/minute-mindfulness-exercises

Lautieri, A. (2019, March 13). Visualization and guided imagery techniques for stress reduction. Mentalhelp.net; admin. https://www.mentalhelp.net/stress/visualization-and-guided-imagery-techniques-for-stress-reduction/

Leavitt, B. (2018, March 6). Shoulds and shouldy thinking. Bill Leavitt Therapist; Bill Leavitt Counseling & Therapy. https://billleavitttherapy.com/shoulds-shouldy-thinking/

Levitt, S. (2023, March 1). What is the difference between a fear and a phobia? Pathways; Pathways Counseling Services. https://www.pathwayscounselingsvcs.com/what-is-the-difference-between-a-fear-and-a-phobia/

Lovering, C. (2016, May 17). 7 best relaxation exercises: Meditation, grounding, and more. Psych Central. https://psychcentral.com/lib/relaxation-exercises-and-techniques

Lukin, K. (2016, September 8). Cognitive behavioral therapy exercises. Lukin Center for Psychotherapy; Lukin Center. https://www.lukincenter.com/5-surprisingly-effective-cognitive-behavioral-therapy-exercises/

Margarita Tartakovsky, M. S. (2016, October 3). Should statements running your life? This might help. Psych Central. https://psychcentral.com/blog/weightless/2016/10/should-statements-running-your-life-this-might-help

May. (2019, May 22). Am I depressed or just sad? Take this quiz to find out. Advantage Care Health Center. https://advantagecaredtc.org/am-i-depressed-or-just-sad/

Mcleod, S., & Evans, O. G. (2022, November 3). Cognitive behavioral therapy (CBT): Types, techniques, uses. Simply Psychology. https://www.simplypsychology.org/cognitive-therapy.html

Millacci, T. S. (2020, October 28). How to relax: Best relaxation techniques for anxiety. Positivepsychology.com. https://positivepsychology.com/relaxation-techniques-anxiety/

Mindful breathing exercises. (2021, March 21). Action for Healthy Kids. https://www.actionforhealthykids.org/activity/mindful-breathing-exercises/

Mooditude. (2021, July 21). Automatic negative thoughts - things you need to know for breaking the habit - mooditude - A happier you! Mooditude - A Happier You! https://mooditude.app/post/automatic-negative-thoughts-things-you-need-to-know-for-breaking-the-habit/

Nicholson, M. (2019, June 5). Safety behaviors. Austin Anxiety Therapists. https://www.austinanxiety.com/safety-behaviors/

Nunez, K. (2020, April 17). ABC model of cognitive behavioral therapy: How it works. Healthline. https://www.healthline.com/health/abc-model

Ohwovoriole, T. (2021, April 13). Understanding Anger. Verywell Mind. https://www.verywellmind.com/what-is-anger-5120208

Perry, E. (n.d.). The purpose of fear and how to overcome it. Betterup.com. https://www.betterup.com/blog/purpose-of-fear

Peterson, A. L. (2019, May 24). What is... A safety behaviour in CBT - mental health @ home. Mental Health @ Home. https://mentalhealthathome.org/2019/05/24/what-is-safety-behaviour/

Pietrangelo, A. (2019, December 12). CBT techniques: Tools for cognitive behavioral therapy. Healthline. https://www.healthline.com/health/cbt-techniques

Positive activities for behavioral activation. (n.d.). Therapist Aid. https://www.therapistaid.com/therapy-worksheet/activities-behavioral-activation/cbt/none

Psychologists, M. (2019, August 12). What are the benefits of cognitive behaviour therapy (CBT)? MyLife Psychologists. https://mylifepsychologists.com.au/what-are-the-benefits-of-cognitive-behaviour-therapy-cbt/

Rabin, P. L. (1983). What is depression? Nephrology Nurse, 5(1), 20–22. https://www.unicef.org/parenting/mental-health/what-is-depression?gclid=CjwKCAjwq4imBhBQEiwA9Nx1BrzSshzQ6LVvMmjM1CfnW2wbY9chnLOeO97HnRR8K1vDD7Ae9YHxPRoCXAQQAvD_BwE

Rachel. (2020, April 21). Black and white thinking: 9 easy ways to stop for good - planning mindfully. Planning Mindfully - Designing Life with Intention. https://www.planningmindfully.com/black-and-white-thinking/

Remez, S. (2021, January 9). 11 benefits of peace of mind and being tranquil. Success Consciousness | Positive Thinking - Personal Development. https://www.successconsciousness.com/blog/inner-peace/benefits-of-peace-of-mind/

Rollo, N. (2019, February 6). Square breathing: How to reduce stress through breathwork. The Couch: A Therapy & Mental Wellness Blog. https://blog.zencare.co/square-breathing/

Roncero, A. (n.d.). Automatic thoughts: How to identify and fix them. Betterup.com. https://www.betterup.com/blog/automatic-thoughts

Self-esteem and teenagers. (n.d.). Reachout.com. https://parents.au.reachout.com/common-concerns/everyday-issues/self-esteem-and-teenagers

Selva, J., & Bc, S. (2018, March 16). Challenging negative automatic thoughts: 5 worksheets (+PDF). Positivepsychology.com. https://positivepsychology.com/challenging-automatic-thoughts-positive-thoughts-worksheets/

Sim, M. (2023, March 9). 25 activities to help your students combat cognitive distortions. Teaching Expertise; dontan. https://www.teachingexpertise.com/classroom-ideas/cognitive-distortions-activity/

Solving problems the cognitive-behavioral way. (n.d.). Psychology Today. https://www.psychologytoday.com/us/blog/all-about-cognitive-and-behavior-therapy/202202/solving-problems-the-cognitive-behavioral-way

Specific phobias. (2023, June 9). Mayo Clinic. https://www.mayoclinic.org/diseases-conditions/specific-phobias/symptoms-causes/syc-20355156

Star, K. (2011, September 13). How "should" statements contribute to panic and anxiety. Verywell Mind. https://www.verywellmind.com/should-statements-2584193

Susan. (2023, January 16). 85 daily affirmations to change your negative thoughts. Sassy Sister Stuff. https://www.sassysisterstuff.com/affirmations-for-negative-thoughts/

Sutton, J. (2020, September 24). 16 decatastrophizing tools, worksheets, and role-plays. Positivepsychology.com. https://positivepsychology.com/decatastrophizing-worksheets/

Sutton, J. (2021, July 24). How to boost self-esteem: 12 simple exercises & CBT tools. Positivepsychology.com. https://positivepsychology.com/self-esteem-boost-exercises/

Teen depression. (2022, August 12). Mayo Clinic. https://www.mayoclinic.org/diseases-conditions/teen-depression/symptoms-causes/syc-20350985

The Depression Project. (2023a, February 10). 75+ positive affirmations for depression. The Depression Project. https://thedepressionproject.com/blogs/news/the-best-positive-affirmations-for-depression

The Depression Project. (2023b, April 5). 3 DBT mindfulness exercises for depression, anxiety & PTSD. The Depression Project. https://thedepressionproject.com/blogs/news/3-dbt-mindfulness-exercises-for-depression-anxiety-ptsd

The difference between fear and phobia. (n.d.). Alliedpsychiatry.com. https://www.alliedpsychiatry.com/blog/the-difference-between-fear-and-phobia

The past, present, and future. (n.d.). Therapistaid.com. https://www.therapistaid.com/worksheets/life-story

The relationship between thoughts, feelings and behaviors. (n.d.). Debbiewoodallcarroll.com. https://debbiewoodallcarroll.com/the-relationship-between-thoughts-feelings-and-behaviors/

Thoughts & behaviors: Costs and benefits. (n.d.). Therapist Aid. https://www.therapistaid.com/therapy-worksheet/cost-benefit-analysis/cbt/adolescents

United We Care. (2023, May 24). The Startling Effects of Anger on Your Mind and Body: Learn more now. United We Care | A Super App for Mental Wellness; United We Care. https://www.unitedwecare.com/the-startling-effects-of-anger-on-your-mind-and-body-learn-more-now/

Using Thought Records to track & challenge thoughts. (2018, April 10). Psychology Tools. https://www.psychologytools.com/self-help/thought-records/

Vallejo, M. (2022, September 7). Mental filter: A cognitive distortion. Mental Health Center Kids. https://mentalhealthcenterkids.com/blogs/articles/mental-filter

Valls, M. (2019, March 7). 10 journal prompts for self-reflection and inner peace. Bee Happi Vintage Press |; Bee Happi Vintage Press. https://beehappi.com/happiness-and-well-being/10-journal-prompts-for-self-reflection-and-inner-peace/

Wagner, K. D. (2016, April 18). 17 affirmations to release negative thoughts. Spirituality+Health. https://www.spiritualityhealth.com/articles/2016/04/18/17-affirmations-release-negative-thoughts

Ward, L. (2021, December 18). 7 yoga poses to inspire your creative side and practice mindful movement. YouAlignedTM. https://youaligned.com/yoga/mindful-movement-yoga-poses/

Weekly schedule for behavioral activation. (n.d.). Therapist Aid. https://www.therapistaid.com/therapy-worksheet/schedule-behavioral-activation/cbt/none

what are emotions? (2015). In What is this thing called Philosophy? (pp. 183–192). Routledge.

What are the benefits of cognitive behavioral therapy (CBT)? (n.d.). Northstartransitions.com. https://www.northstartransitions.com/post/what-are-the-benefits-of-cognitive-behavioral-therapy-cbt

What is anger? Definition & psychology behind this emotion. (n.d.). Betterhelp.com. https://www.betterhelp.com/advice/anger/what-is-anger-definition-psychology-behind-this-emotion/

What is behaviour? - Principles for effective support. (n.d.). Gov.au. https://www.health.nsw.gov.au/mentalhealth/psychosocial/principles/Pages/behaviour-whatis.aspx

What is fear? (2019, September 17). Paul Ekman Group. https://www.paulekman.com/universal-emotions/what-is-fear/

What is mindfulness? (2020). In Building and Sustaining a Teaching Career (pp. 15–28). Cambridge University Press.

What is the Cognitive Triangle and How is it Used? (2021, September 13). KASA Solutions. https://kasa-solutions.com/what-is-the-cognitive-triangle-and-how-is-it-used/

Williams, A. J. (n.d.). A quote from The Psychic Mind. Goodreads.com. https://www.goodreads.com/quotes/1344024-thoughts-create-emotions-emotions-create-feelings-and-feelings-create-behaviour

Williamson, T. (2021, June 1). 10 breathing exercises for kids with anxiety or anger. Mindfulmazing.com; Mindfulmazing. https://www.mindfulmazing.com/10-breathing-exercises-for-kids-with-anxiety-or-anger/

Wood, K. (2020, November 9). The connection between thoughts and emotions. Kamini Wood. https://www.kaminiwood.com/the-connection-between-thoughts-and-emotions/

Worry exploration questions. (n.d.). Therapist Aid. https://www.therapistaid.com/therapy-worksheet/worry-exploration-questions/cbt/adolescents

Zayed, A. (2022, November 1). 4 Benefits of Cognitive behavioral therapy. The Diamond Rehab Thailand; Theo de Vries. https://diamondrehabthailand.com/cognitive-behavioral-therapy-benefits/

Zorbas, A. (2021, July 30). Should statements: Reframe the way you think. Therapy Now. https://www.therapynowsf.com/blog/should-statements-reframe-the-way-you-think

Carol. (2022, April 30). Mental filtering: What to know about this cognitive distortion. A Cognitive Connection. https://acognitiveconnection.com/cognitive-distortion-mental-filtering/

Rebecca Joy Stanborough, M. F. A. (2020, February 4). Cognitive restructuring: Techniques and examples. Healthline. https://www.healthline.com/health/cognitive-restructuring

(N.d.). Choosingtherapy.com. Retrieved August 20, 2023, from https://www.choosingtherapy.com/cognitive-restructuring/

www.ingramcontent.com/pod-product-compliance
Lightning Source LLC
Chambersburg PA
CBHW060414010526
44107CB00006B/687